Public Sector Banks In India

And

Liberalisation

Sanjaykumar Durgabhai Paramar

Jagdishbhai Ambalal Parmar

Publish World

2013

Price : $27.86

First Edition : 2013

ISBN : 978-0-9921545-7-8

Publisher ISBN Prefix : 978-0-9921545

ISBN Allotment Agency : Library and Archives Canada (Govt. of Canada)

Published & Printed by

Publish World
81, Woodlot Crescent,
Etobicoke,
Toronto, Ontario, Canada.
Postal Code- M9W 6T3
Phone- +1 (647) 633 9712
http://www.publishworld.org

ACKNOWLEDGEMENT

We would like to thank our family members as well as our colleagues who have inspired us to write this book.

We have immense pleasure to dedicate this book to

1. Dr. H.P. Trivedi
2. Dr. N.M. Patel
3. Prof. Gaurang Desai

They have provided their precious blessing for the publication of book.

- Sanjaykumar D. Paramar

- Jagdishbhai A. Parmar

PREFACE

In the Indian context, banking is really the proxy and indeed the corner stone of overall economic growth of the country. According to C.H. Bhabha, "Banking is the kingpin of the chariot of economic progress. As such its role in expanding economy of a country like India can neither be underestimated nor overlooked. The success of our plan is dependent among other things, on the smooth and satisfactory performance of the role by banking industry of our country." Banking is a service-oriented business requiring high levels of professional and personal skills and national boundaries are no longer relevant in mobilization and allocation of capital.

The Indian banking industry has come from a long way from being passive business institution to a highly proactive and dynamic entity. Before liberalization, the Indian banking structure was largely controlled and parameters like branch size and location were given much importance. Presently, the Indian banking industry is going through a period of intense change, where liberalized business environment has affected the banking business by way of increasing competition, rising customer expectations, shrinking spreads and increasing disintermediation. Public sector banks largely dominate the Indian banking industry; however, their share has been declining. Their inefficiencies came into picture only when the market was thrown open for competition and new glares started eating up their share. The setting up of a new competitive environment has resulted in new challenges for the public sector banks to retain their share. Ongoing changes in the structure of Indian banking are clearly visible. While the share of public sector banks in the total assets of the banking sector has shown a steady decline, the new private sector banks and foreign banks have succeeded in enhancing their position.

No doubt, PSBs have strong distribution network all over the country. But the strength of the earlier periods has now become a concern for these banks. As compare to the tech-equipped distribution network of the new private sector banks and foreign banks, these banks have found it difficult to upgrade them on the technology front. PSBs have started embracing technology to improve customer service and design innovative products to increase sales opportunities. In the face of increased competition, public sector banks have also started undertaking various cost-reduction programmes. These banks are also facing the problem of surplus manpower.

Most of these banks came out with VRS to bring down their number of employees and improve the productivity ratios. The foreign banks too have been facing stiff competition from the new private banks. Some of the top foreign banks have also lost their individual shares. In the face of growing competition, the policy changes and the operational environment in respect of the Indian banking system, there has been an increased focus on profitability, although other social objectives continue to be important. Consequently, most of the banks in the public sector have shown a significant improvement in their profit performance. The profit performance has been quite varied among different bank groups and within each group in respect of individual banks as well. Generally, new private sector banks and foreign banks have performed better than public sector banks and old private sector banks in most of the years of the study period. While the level of Non-Performing Assets of public sector banks remains high, a noteworthy development has been their significant reduction in relation to net advances in recent years. In order to remain in the competition, it is required to convert the challenge of change into exciting opportunity.

The present study is an attempt to have an idea of the impact of liberalization on the productivity and profitability of public sector banks in India. For the purpose of study the relevant data has been collected for the period of 12 years. The variables considered for the performance appraisal of banks include various per branch and per employee indicators apart from various other profitability ratios. It has been found that the overall performance of PSBs has not improved much. But it is worth mentioning here that various innovative steps by PSBs have shown that in the future, these banks can regain their lost position to a large extent, if not fully. Therefore, the future is going to be tough for every player in the banking sector.

CONTENTS

CONTENTS

CHAPTER – I
INTRODUCTION

Introduction

The main challenge before a developing nation is to foster sustainable growth. For growth or its recovery, the nation's productive capacity has to be strengthened and expanded. In the development agenda, an important issue relates to the problem of the provision and delivery of the financial service and credit. Banking is the fulcrum of an Economy. The Banking Industry is one of the basic instruments of economic growth. It must be on a sound footing as it constitutes an important link in various socio-economic activities. Since it is considered the backbone of economic development, any change in its processes is deemed to have repercussions on the country's growth. The essential part of the banking system is its financial viability. It is not only necessary for its survival but also to discharge its various obligations.

Traditionally, Indian Banking Systems operated primarily in the private sector. From very ancient days, indigenous banking as different from the modern Western Banking had been organized in the form of family or individual business. The basic inability of the Indian Banking Sector to help, develop the economy and serve the society to the desired level, led to a demand for restructuring of the banking system. But it was only in 1931 that the Central Banking Enquiry Committee asked for linking the prevalent banking business with RBI. In this way, traditional Indian banking system operated primarily in private sector. Until nationalization, the banking system had more or less confined its activities to different classes of people and thus, helped only big borrowers.

The Imperial Bank of India was nationalized and its undertaking was taken over by the State Bank of India (SBI) in 1955. It was done for the purpose of imposing social control with a view to remedy the basic weaknesses of the Indian banking system and to ensure that banks would cater to the needs of the hither to neglect and weaker sections of community instead of big business and those connected with them. On July 19, 1969, 14 major banks and on April 15, 1980, six banks were nationalized. The object other nationalization was to render the largest good to the largest number of people. The present scheduled banking structure has been depicted in the Figure 1.1. From the figure, it becomes clear that there are 27 public sector banks operating in India. Apart from 32 private sector banks, 42 foreign

1

banks and 196 RRBs. In addition to that there are 57 scheduled urban cooperative banks and 16 scheduled state cooperative banks. Out of the 27 public sector banks, there are 19 nationalized banks and others are SBI and its associates.

The present structure of the Indian commercial banks has been shown in the Table 1.1. From the table it is clear that the major share as far as deposits and advances are concerned, is enjoyed by the public sector banks in India. However a noteworthy point here is that the share has been continuously declining over the period under study and new generation private sector banks and foreign banks are taking away their shares. In the total assets of the Indian commercial banks the share of public sector banks was 72.92 per cent in the year 2003 which was much higher in the earlier years.

Table 1.1

Structure of Indian Commercial Banks (2003) (Rs. In crore)

S. No.	Bank Group	No. of Banks	Deposits	Capital	Reserves	Total Assets	Borrowings	Investments	Loan and Advances
1.	Public Sector Banks	27	1079393.81	14175.39	51407.16	128235.70	22431.04	545668.10	549351.18
	Market Share	9.34	76.87	59.30	65.37	72.92	25.60	77.26	72.07
2.	Indian Private Sector	30	207173.57	2921.06	15974.40	297279.31	42139.95	107327.94	138951.10
	Banks Market Share	10.38	14.75	12.22	20.31	16.87	48.10	15.20	18.23
3.	Foreign Banks in Indian	36	69312.82	4497.79	8906.28	116401.08	22904.42	40795.49	52170.87
	Market Share	12.46	4.94	18.82	11.32	6.60	26.14	5.78	6.84
4.	Total Private Sector	66	276486.39	7418.85	24880.68	413680.39	65044.37	148123.53	191121.97
	Banks Market Share	22.84	19.69	31.04	31.64	23.47	74.25	20.97	25.07
5.	TotalCommercial Banks	93	1355880.20	21594.24	76287.84	1698916.09	87475.41	693791.53	740473.15
	Market Share	32.18	96.56	90.34	97.00	96.39	99.85	98.23	97.14
6.	Regional Rural Banks	196 67.82	48338.00	2308.59	2357.41	63614.00	131.00	12524.00	21773.00
	Market Share		3.44	9.66	3.00	3.61	0.15	1.77	2.86
7.	Total of All Banks	289	1404218.20	23902.83	78645.25	1762530.09	87606.41	706315.53	762246.15
	Total Market Share	100.00	100.00	100.00	100.00	100.00	100.00	100.00	100.00

Source: *RBI's Report on Trend and Progress of Banking in India (2002-03)*

Role of Banks in Economic Development

Banks play a very significant role in the economic development of a country. Banks have control over a major part of the supply of money in circulation. In this way, they can influence the nature and character of production in the country. In fact, banks are the main stay of the economic development of a country.

Figure 1.2

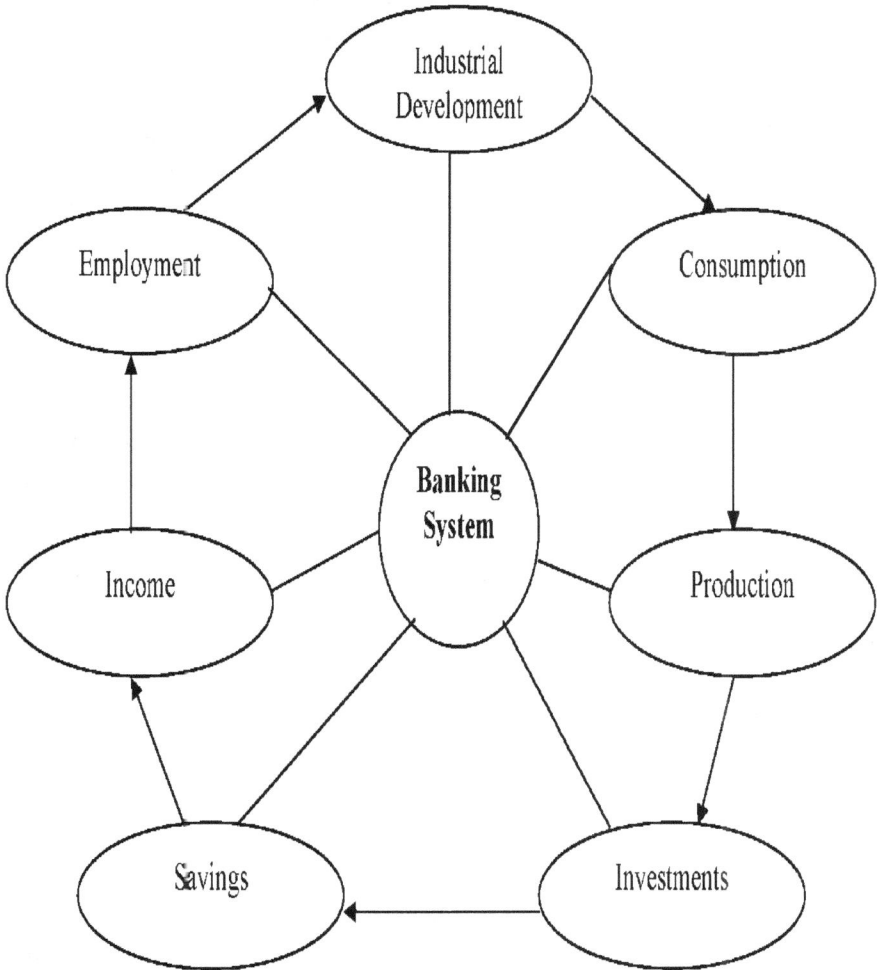

Industrial Development

Employment

Consumption

Banking System

Income

Production

Savings

Investments

Economic Development through Banking System

The contribution of the banking sector in the process of economic development can be summarized as under:

1. Banks help in Capital Formation: Banks mobilize the idle and dormant capital of a community and make it available for productive purposes. In fact, banks have designed a number of schemes to attract the prospective customers to encourage the habit of savings among the people.
2. Banks are the Creator of Money: Banks are described as factories of credit. They have the power to create money and it helps in the economic development of the country.
3. Banks act as a link between the organized and unorganized sectors: In India, money market consists of organized and unorganized sectors. Both of them are required to be linked for economic development of the country and this function is performed by banks.
4. Banks help in the effective implementation of monetary policy:
5. The effective implementation of monetary policy can be done only through properly organized banking system of the country.
6. Banks help in the development of agriculture and industries: The development of a country not only depends upon the industrial development but also on development of agriculture. The banks cater to the financial needs of these sectors which result in the economic development of the country.
7. Banks act as catalyst in social change: In India banks are regarded as catalysts in bringing the desired social change in community. Banks are able to achieve the desired change through it sectoral priorities and other social development programmers.
8. Banks help in the development of entrepreneurship: Banks have special drives and specific schemes for the development of entrepreneurship. Banks help in boosting their strength and health.

9. Banks regulate the flow of national savings: Banks regulate the flow of national savings. They ensure the diversion of national savings into productive purposes.
10. Banks help in mitigating the effects of trade cycles:
11. The effective banking system can help the government in controlling the circulation of money. It helps in mitigating the effects of trade cycles in a country.
12. Banks help in maintaining the positive balance of trade:Banks also help in promoting import and maintaining the balance of trade at favourable position.

From the above, it became clear that the banking system occupies an important position in an economy. Bankers are regarded as, "Public Conservators of Commercial Virtues." A country with an effective banking system has a secure foundation of economic development.

It is a fact that in order to judge the financial maturity, the size of bank assets of the economy plays an active role. The size of bank assets in relation to GDP has important implications for the financial development of any economy.

The nationalization of the banks bestowed upon them variety of new obligations in the area of social banking. The major achievements of the nationalized banks are in the sphere of branch, expansion deposit mobilization and expansion of credit to heather to neglect sectors which are important for the national economy in terms of their contribution to the growth, employment generation and broadening the base of income distribution.

After the nationalization of banks, the major concern was the productivity and profitability of public sector banks. It was believed that the new direction given to the banks since their nationalization in 1969, and the slacking productivity, has led to declining trends in the profits and profitability. It is even held that unless the present trend is reversed, the financial viability of our banking system may be undermined. It was confirmed by the Narasimham Report in 1991, which stated the bank' profitability has been under severe stress.

But the banking system must be on a sound footing not only to instill public confidence but also to make banks capable of discharging their social responsibility. A number of facors like the entry of the overseas financial intermediaries into domestic financial markets necessitated some kinds of charges. Banking sector being the heart line of the financial market, their upgradation and financial strength is more vital for an efficient financial system. With these views, RBI and Government had initiated the process of banks reforms by setting up Narasimham Committee 1 in 1991. Thus the bank reforms heralded the beginning of implementing prudential norms consisting of capital adequacy ratio, asset classification, income recognition, and provisioning. Broadly, banking sector reforms have been concerned with improving.

1. The policy framework,
2. The financial health, and The institutional infrastructure.

In the Indian context, banking is really the mirror of economic growth of the country. Before liberalization, the Indian banking structure was largely controlled and parameters like branch size and location were given paramount importance. The Indian banking industry has come from a long way from being a sleepy business institution to a highly proactive and dynamic entity. Now, the Indian banking industry is going through a period of intense change, where global trends are affecting the banking business increasing competition, liberalization, rising customer expectations, shrinking spreads, increasing disintermediation, competitive prizing and possibilities macro-volatility. This transformation has been largely brought about by the large dose of liberalization and economic reforms.

Banks reports and worry about non-performing assets and are visibly grappling with an increasingly competitive environment. The importance of primary capital markets in the mid-1990, threatened banks with disintermediation and the rise of non-banking finance companies threaten them in the business of deposit mobilization itself. The focus of public attention has mostly been on the banking sector's ability to meet these challenges. New entrants are able to take advantage of the benefits of latest technology and adopt business models to leapfrog ahead. Increasing inroads from non-traditional players are being witnessed. The intense competitive retain environment forcing banks to increasing become customer-centric. Banks are embracing technology to improve customer service; design flexible and customized products increase sales opportunities and differentiate themselves in a market where product features are easily cloned. Indian banking system is quite matured today. Needless to say future is going to full of challenges. Therefore, it is

6

required to convert the challenge of change into exciting opportunity. Now, new horizons are sought and new challenges encountered. Banking is a service-oriented business requiring high levels of professional and personal skills and national boundaries are no longer relevant in mobilization and allocation of capital. The public sector banks largely dominate the Indian banking industry. These banks till the early-1990s were involved in the traditional banking business of deposits and credit - lending. They performed a sportive role in the overall growth of the economy.

The root cause for the lackluster performance of banks formed the elements of the banking sector reforms. The need for the restructuring the bank industry was felt greater with the initiation of the real sector reforms process in 1992. It is because to harness the benefits of globalization. There should be an efficient financial sector to support the structural reforms take place in the real economy. The foundation of the banking sector reforms was laid down by M. Narasimham Committee on financial sector reforms. Causal factors for dismissal performance were addressed. To bring about a paradigm shift in the banking sector, the financial sector reforms were initiated.

Implications of the Reforms for the Banking Sector

1)   Entry barriers were lowered.
2)   Interest rates were deregulated.
3)   Regulation w.r.t. Branch licensing, credit control, approach to capital market were lowered.
4)   The prudential norms were introduced w.r.t. income recognition, asset classification, and provision, capital adequacy to strengthen the banks balance and enhance the transparency.

In fact, the main aim of these regulations was to induce the financial discipline into the operations. The reform measures were not only aimed at liberalizing the regulatory framework but also to keep them in tune with international standards. Further, regulations aimed at enhancing the transparency and accountability in the operations of the banks is to support the economic growth while the productivity and the profitability do not take back seat in that set up.

To strengthen the banking system in general and public sector banks in particularly, the institution building measures taken are

1. Recapitalization,
2. Improving the quality of the loan portfolio,.
3. Instilling a greater element of competition, and
4. Strengthening the supervisory process.

The Indian Banking Industry is full of competition, due to liberalization. The players are competing like never before. Yesterdays stars are no longer stars, new stars are emerging on the scene.

Now banks have performed better than others to keep ahead in race. So there has arisen a need to improve the performance level lest the banks are likely to be left far behind. It is imperative to know the terms which have been used widely in the study. These are:

Liberalization

Liberalisation involves freeing prizes, trade and entry from state controls. In fact, the degree to which an economy is free can be defined by scope of state involvement, either directly by ownership or indirectly by regulation, in markets for products or services. Liberalization does not raise real interests and results in an increased diversity of financial instruments. Unwary investors may be taken by the rather fanciful terms offered. In fact, as a result of liberalization, now there is a pressure on profits and portability of public sector banks. It can lead to speculation and create problems of systematic failures. In fact, liberalization and deregulation encompasses the following:

1. Interest rate and other price deregulation measures.
2. Removal of direct credit controls and mandatory investment regulations.
3. Measures design to promote entry of new competitors.
4. Supportive merger and ownership policy.
5. Prudential regulation and reliance on indirect tools for controls, and
6. Transparency.

Productivity

Productivity is a vital indicator of economic performance. In simple words, it is output-input ratio. It is a relationship between given output and the means used to produce it. Banking is primarily a service industry. There are number of indicators to measure the productivity of banking sector. Measures of productivity at bank or industry level may differ from the indicators of productivity at branch level.

Productivity is affected by man power, mechanization, system and the procedures, costing of operations, customer services and various external aspects. There are number of ratios of compute productivity as:

Per Employee Indicators (Labour Productivity):
(1)   Deposit per employee
(2)   Advance per employee
(3)   Business per employee
(4)   Total expenditure per employee
(5)   Total income per employee
(6)   Spread per employee
(7)   Net profit per employee
(8)   Burden per employee

Per Branch Indicators (Branch Productivity):
(1)   Deposits per branch
(2)   Advance per branch
(3)   Business per branch
(4)   Total income per branch
(5)   Total expenditure per branch
(6)   Burden per branch
(7)   Net profit per branch Spread per branch

Profitability

Profitability is a rate expressing profit as a percentage of total assets or sales or any other variable to represent the relationship. In fact, there may be various dimensions of profitability analysis. A large number of ratios can be used in order to measure the banks profitability as:
1.   Interest Income to Working Funds Ratio
2.   Interest Expended to Working Funds Ratio
3.   Spread to Working Funds Ratio

4. Non-Interest Income to Working Funds Ratio
5. Non-Interest Expenditure to Working Funds Ratio
6. Burden to Working Funds Ratio
7. Net Profit to Working Funds Ratio
8. Interest Income to Total Income Ratio
9. Interest Expended to Total Expenditure Ratio
10. Staff Expenditure to Operating Expenditure Ratio.

Need and Scope of the Study

The PSBs account for the major share of banking business in this country. But the PSBs are functioning under pressure from government, regulatory agencies, and the public. The reform process started in 1991 poses challenges before bankers as never before. After liberalization, various new private sector banks and foreign banks have joined the banking industry in India. It is generally belived that there is a decline in profitability and productivity of the PSBs as a result of liberalization. It is believed that PSBs have not only lost their deposits to new generation private sector banks but also to old private sector banks and foreign sector banks. Only four banks, *viz.* State Bank of India, Bank of Baroda, Punjab National Bank, Canara Bank had more than 5 per cent market share in March, 1999. PSBs witnessed substantial loss in their market share deposit and still are losing, will have really struggle for retaining their position in the next millennium. So, there is need to have a look on PSBs for post-liberalization period.

As far as scope of the study is concerned, it covers all the 27 PSBs functioning in India. These are:

1. Allahabad Bank
2. Andhra Bank
3. Bank of Baroda
4. Bank of India
5. Bank of Maharashtra
6. Canara Bank
7. Central Bank of India
8. Corporation Bank
9. Dena Bank
10. Indian Bank
11. Indian Overseas Bank

10

12. Oriented Bank of Commerce

13. Punjab and Sindh Bank

14. Punjab National Bank

15. State Bank of Bikaner and Jaipur

16. State Bank of Hyderabad

17. State Bank of Indore

18. State Bank of Mysore

19. State Bank of Patiala

20. State Bank of Saurashtra

21. State Bank of Travancore

22. State Bank of India

23. Syndicate Bank

24. United Commercial Bank

25. Union Bank of India

26. United Bank of India
27. Vijaya Bank

The period of the study is 12 years spanning from 1996 to 2007. As observed from the review of the literature, no study has been carried out regarding the impact of liberalization on the productivity and profitability of public sector banks so it becomes imperative to know the impact. Studies which have been carried out prior to liberalization are related to one or the other aspect of public sector banks. Even the researches carried out in the post-liberalization period ignored this important aspect and failed to give the variables and their impact on PSBs. The derivations of studies in pre-liberalisation period are going to be used as per as the requirements of the present study.

Banking needs to be looked at from the relevance of the Indian economy. Whatever the economy goes through, banks have a significant role to play. Presently, there are 32 private banks and 42 foreign banks operating in the country besides public sector banks which mop up the bulk of the banking business, which accounts for 76 per cent of the total deposits and 72 per cent of the total advances. Presently, this sector contributes about 8 per cent to the GDP of the economy.

The public sector banks have strong distribution network all over the country. But the strength of the earlier periods has now become a concern for these banks. As compared to the tech-equipped distribution network of the new private sector banks and foreign banks, these banks have found it difficult to upgrade them on the technology front. These banks are also facing the problem of surplus manpower. Most of these banks have coming out with VRS to bring down their number of employees and improve the efficiency ratios.

The inefficiencies of PSBs were exposed only when the market was thrown open for competition and new glares started eating up their share. But given their size and strong network, most of these can change their perception. Since the growth of economy is largely dependent on the performance of these banks, even with the growth of new private and foreign players, these banks will have an important role to play.

The economic liberalization process has increasingly exposed Indian industry to international competition and in case of some industries; this has greatly sequenced their margins rendering them in capable of repaying the loans taken by them from banks, with the deficiencies noticed in managing credit risks.

The winds of liberalization have opened up new vistas in the banking industry resulting in the generation of intensely competitive environment. The banking areas have been almost completely flooded with new entrants including private banks, foreign banks, non-banking finance companies (NBFCs), the merchant bankers and chit funds etc. The foreign banks and new private sector banks have spearhead the hi-tech the revolution mainly targeted at the cream corporate-clientele of banks.

Objectives of the Study
The broad objectives of this study are as under:
- To evaluate profitability and productivity of PSBs in the *viz-a-viz* post-liberalization period.
- To identify the various factors affecting the profitability and productivity of PSBs in the post- liberalization period.

- To examine the contribution of various factors towards the profitability and productivity of PSBs in the *viz-a-viz* post-liberalization period.
- To make suggestions or the improvement in the profitability and productivity of PSBs.
- To create platform for future research in this area.
- The productivity and profitability of PSBs has suffered in the post-liberalization period.
- There has been a change in the nature of the factors affecting the productivity and profitability of PSBs in the post-liberalization period.
- Various new generation private and foreign banks have posed a great challenge to PSBs in the post- liberalisatiion period by introducing various innovative schemes.
- Various PSBs have started various innovative schemes, hitherto unknown even to the private sector banks.

CHAPTER – II

LIBERALIZATION

Liberalization

Change is the law of nature. Nothing in the world is permanent except change. Everything is bound to change in this world. Banking is no exception to this general rule. Modern era is the era of globalization and liberalization. The trend towards globalization worldwide began towards the end of 1960. The subsequent oil crisis, coupled with the need of circumvents regulatory restrictions, led to the development of Euro currencies. These were in sense precursors to free markets. The floating of the US dollar in 1971 marked the break not only with the system of regulated exchange design but also Keynesian ideology that dependent on state action for employment generation. There was a buildup of resentment against the ever rising costs of the welfare measures and their misuse. The rather poor performance of the public sector units also helped in building up a strong opinion against state intervention.

Changes in the economic environment affect relations between financial and non-financial corporations, between government and financial/non-financial institutions and thus between polity and economy. Any change process involves changing not just one particular thing, but necessitates a series of changes at different places. The same premise holds good in the world of banking also.

Globalization covers a wide spectrum like expanding international trade, growth of multinational business, rise in international joint ventures, and movement of labour and increasing independence through capital flows. Today markets are no longer synonymous with geographical coordinates. Countries do not produce all at home but the world is perceived as a global village where resources are best utilized at source and value additions done there.

The spirit of globalization is very rightly reflected in Kenichi Ohmae's words: "Being a global player means viewing the whole global market as your proper soil, your place to plant trees and nourish them. No matter what happens to a particular tree, you do not even think of transplanting the rest - not if the soil is right and the weather is mostly fine. They will bear fruit in another season, if not this year."

14

Liberalizations Defined

Liberalizations and deregulation connote different things to different scholars even in the same group. To some it is just another name of privatization. To other it meant a dilution of Reserve Bank or Finance Ministry control. In banking it is concerned with policy changes and equating this with the reform process. In fact, liberalization involves freeing prizes, trade and entry from state controls. Further, free markets do not mean a complete way to markets. The degree to which an economy is free can be defined by the scope of state involvement, either directly by ownership or indirectly by regulation, in markets for products or services.

Liberalization does not mean that each and every player should establish offices elsewhere. This is not liberalisatiion. In fact, liberalization is a mental attitude. Liberalisation is a process by which the economy is opened up and stringent regulatory measures are relaxed to a large extent. Earlier no player ever thought of opening a branch in other countries market as there was absolutely no role to play in any of those markets. Now everyone has acquired a global perspective.

Liberalisation is not simply allowing the foreigners to access the vast potential of the Indian market. Actually it is concerned with opening of the markets which have immense potential, but this perspective is a limited perspective and we should go beyond it. We should not look at liberalization from that limited perspective, *viz.* opening up the markets.

Presently in the case of PSBs, there is low productivity, low profitability and low morale and it is not possible for PSBs to enter the international market and think in the terms of doing business internationally. Only by improving their functioning PSBs can really equate themselves with any international bank and think in terms of competing with them in the international market place. If they do not change their working style, they cannot operate even in their own country as they will be swallowed by some strong international banking institution in the near future.

Indian banking sector should recognize the business process re-engineering. Only after adopting a business process re-engineering in proper shape and matching the work flow to meet their customer service needs, PSBs can develop the technology and stay with that technology in the future.

Various drastic changes are taking place the world-over and attention has been focused on liberalisation and deregulation. The main objective is to give a greater role to market forces in improving allocative efficiency, removing distortions caused by unrealistic pricing, strengthening the viability of financial institutions to enable them to compete and withstand disintermediation and to create, competitive environment conducive to innovation and growth. With the lowering of trade barriers and growing cross-border flows, markets are becoming global, and profitability and productivity have become the cornerstones.

After a survey of experiences of financial sector reform in nine Asian countries, Tseng and Corker concluded that overall financial liberalization and monitory policy reform have contributed to more efficient financial systems and have enhanced the effectiveness and flexibility of monitory policy[1].

The most distinguishing feature, however, is growing internationalization and integration of financial markets the world over, accompanied by greater institutionalization of saving and a broader and increasingly complex range of financial instruments. Advances in information technology and communication accompanied by the increased ability to transform risks have led to the integration of financial markets worldwide, with funds flowing from surplus areas to those with investment opportunity.

The process of liberalization and globalization has become a driving force for modern economic development throughout the world. Both the developed and the developing economies have been initiating suitable reform measures in order to make their economies more vibrant and strategically competitive. In India, with a view to gaining the twin goals of macro economic stabilization and structural adjustments, the process of reforms - fiscal, financial, monetary and industrial - was set in motion with great zeal in mid-1991. Owing to these reforms the entire competitive structure of the economic system has witnessed a major change. The banking sector reforms being an integral part of financial reforms aim at making banks much more internally viable and internationally competitive. The demarcation line between the banking and financial institutions *viz-a-viz* non-banking financial institutions has become significantly thin. Competition has become more intense and diversified. The entry of foreign banks and new private sector banks has increased competitiveness and cost consciousness among the PSBs. The various dimensions of financial liberalization are:

- Abolishing credit controls.
- Deregulating interest rates.
- Allowing free entry into the banking industry or more generally into financial services industry.
- Making banks autonomous.
- Putting banks in private ownership.
- Freeing international capital flows.

Liberalization in Financial Services

In a very wide context one could describe the policy changes as market-oriented. It not only relates to policies dealing with restrictive business practices, concentration, dominant market position and cooperative/informal cartel agreements, but also covers all measures that are designed to encourage and provide more scope for the working of market forces and for competition in banking and finance. Thus a wide range of domestic deregulation measures as well as external liberalization measures are considered as falling within the scope of these policies.

The external debt crisis, which surfaced in early-1991, brought India close to default in meeting its international payments obligations. The balance of payments situation was almost unmanageable. Indian deregulation exercise was initiated by the owners and was inspired from the top as a response to a crisis situation.

The financial sector reforms were initiated to bring about a paradigm shift in the banking industry. In this context, the recommendations made by a high level committee on financial sector, chaired by M. Narasimham, laid the foundation for the banking sector reforms. The Committee, which was set up in 1991, submitted its report in 1992. Another committee was constituted under the chairmanship of M. Narasimham which submitted its report in 1998.

These reforms tried to enhance the viability and efficiency of the banking sector. To tackle the internal deficiencies of the sector, new norms relating to accounting practices, prudential standards and capital adequacy requirements were suggested. On the other hand, for improving the external environment, the reforms aimed to transform the highly regulated environment into a market-oriented one.

While most of the recommendations made by the Narsimham Committee have been accepted for implementation, either in a single step or in phased manner, some of them were not adopted in a satisfactory way. The measures implemented so far have revolutionalized the structure of the banking industry and its operations.

The major policy thrust is to improve the operational and allocative efficiency of the financial system as a whole by correcting many of the exogenous and structural factors affecting the performance of financial institutions. Easing of external constraints such as administered interest rate structures and reserve requirements for banks, strengthening the capital base of financial institutions, facilitating the entry of new institutions, exploring in direct monetary policy instruments, and strengthening prudential regulations can be said to be the gist of financial sector reforms.

Problems with Liberalization

It would be incorrect to expect that liberalization and deregulation will solve all problems just by the initiation of these relaxed policies, it is not so. The major problems concerned with liberalization can be summarized as under:

(1)   In so far as fiscal deficits are financed by money creation and growing, financial liberalization serves to accelerate inflation which coupled with an over- valued exchange rate, promotes capital flight.

(2)   Liberalisation does raise real interests and results in an increased diversity of financial instruments. Innocent investors may be taken in by the rather fanciful terms offered.

(3)   Competition is not automatically enhanced. It can lead to domination by big institution that has market controlling powers.

(4)   Distortions in credit allocation or self dealing by banks can produce efficiency gains.

(5)   Deregulation can shorten the horizons of savers and investors, leading to a drawing up of long-term finance.

(6)   Sometimes there can be problems of moral hazard.

(7)   Pressure on profits and profitability can lead to speculation and create problems of systemic failures.

(8)   With fewer entry restrictions, it has been possible for many entrants to make inroads into this lucrative sector, some antisocial elements can enter the field directly or indirectly.

(9) A number of companies can incorporate their own finance companies to make finance available on easy terms for purchase of their products, this phenomenon can also be used against the interest of the society.

But it must be noticed that careless liberalization, rather than careful liberalization has often been the real culprit. Although the banking sector played a crucial role in widening its reach, its own health had got impaired, Low operational efficiency contributed to low profitability and consequently to erosion of its capital base. Therefore reforms in the banking sector were really required. Reforms were directed, among others at the gradual reduction in the pre-emption of resources of banks, institutional strengthening, rationalization of the interest rate structure, imparting greater competition through entry of new banks.

Convergence in the banking sector assumes increased significance because banks today no longer compete nearly with other banks. They, in fact, compete with altogether different sectors. The only problem of banking sector is likely to face the process of integration is the relative lack of service costing culture in the country. The banking sector will need to give due care to activity-based costing to be able to load their overheads across their products and services scientifically. This also presents the danger that the banks may move away from lending to sectors that need banking support not because these sectors are intrinsically unprofitable but because their profitability is not captured properly.

One argument against liberalization has been that it could lead banks to lend at higher and higher rates of interest and thereby accept high levels of risk. This phenomenon can be defined as a process of "adverse selection." In fact, the answer to adverse selection is the prescription of prudential norms, which will compel banks not to accept risks beyond a point.

Survival of the fittest in the age of cut-throat competition is the statement which aptly describes the present state of banking industry. Ever since the Narsimham Committee recommendations were put into practice, the banking sector has undergone a metamorphosis change. From reduction of barriers for entry of PSBs to deregulation of interest rates on deposits and advances to introduction of capital adequacy norms the banking sector reforms have come a long way. The banking industry is facing competition from both within and outside, from the new generation private sector banks, foreign banks, FIs as well as NBFCs. Evidence of increased competition emerges from changes in the market shares between public and private sector banks, competition in the quality and range of services offered etc.

It should also be noticed that liberalization can also result in the increase in instability. In general, financial liberalization represents a profound change in the economic rules. It can "increase the riskiness of traditional behaviour or introduce new inexperienced players." In these circumstances, disasters can also take place.

Advantages of Liberalization

Liberalisation can well be considered an investment in the future financial well being of a nation. It helps the banking industry as a whole by providing:

1. Increased financial flexibilities of firms.
2. Reduced transaction costs.
3. Improved allocation efficiency.
4. Attraction of new capital to financial intermediaries.
5. Stronger and more competitive banking institutions.
6. Better and diversified portfolios.
7. More effective conduct of monetary policy.
8. Meaningful competition in banking services by allowing greater role to private sector and foreign banks.
9. Technological up-gradation of banks through wide use of computers and modern communication systems.
10. Removing major regulatory impediments to profitable working of banks.
11. Relaxation in the regulations covering foreign investment and foreign exchange.
12. Easy access to foreign capital.

The financial sector, following liberalization has seen several firms from abroad entering into strategic alliances with Indian companies *e.g.,* ICICI and JP Morgan, DSP Financial Services and Merrill Lynch, Kotak Mahindra etc. It must be noticed that international trade and global strategies call for global financial relationship. As the Indian financial system gets integrated with the financial markets, a massive growth of large value funds transfers will take place. Banking must have systems ready to support the flows. Top quality services must be offered at a competitive price. With MNCs becoming more powerful and influential in their countries of operations, there is a need for entering into strategic alliances or establishing presence abroad through foreign subsidiaries where possible.

While nationalization achieved the widening of the banking industry in India, the task of deepening their services was still left unattended. By the beginning of 1990, the social banking goals set for the banking industry made most of the public sector banks unprofitable. The fact that majority of the banks were in public sector resulted in the presumption that there was no need to look at the fundamental financial strength of these banks. Consequently, they remained undercapitalized. Revamping this structure of the banking industry was of extreme importance, as the health of the financial sector in particular and the economy as a whole would be reflected by its performance.

The need for restructuring the banking industry was felt greater with the initiation of the real sector reform process in 1992. The reforms have enhanced the opportunities and challenges for the real sector making them operate in a borderless global market place. However, to enjoy the benefits of liberalization, there should be an efficient financial sector to support the structural reforms taking place in the real economy. Hence along with the reforms of the real sector, the banking sector reforms were started.[3]

The main cause for the lackluster performance of banks which formed the elements of the banking sector reforms were:
1. Greater Emphasis on Directed Credit;
2. Regulated Interest Rate Structure;
3. Lack of Focus On Profitability;
4. Lack of Transparency In The Banks Balance Sheet;
5. Lack of Competition;
6. Lack of Grasp Of The Risks Involved;
7. Excessive Regulations on Organization Structure And Managerial Resource;
8. Excessive Support From Government;
9. Excessive Focus On Quantitative Achievements;

Impact of Liberalizations on Banking

The banking sector in India has remained regulated since nationalization in 1969. Private bank entry was restricted after nationalization to prevent unfair competition, urban concentration and lending to rich and well known firms. This resulted in elimination of competition among public sector banks, public-private sector banks. There was a reduction in efficiency in performance and the decline in quality of customer service. Soon after nationalization commercial banks were asked to cater the needs of priority sector. Since 1969 the interest rates in India have been set by the Reserve Bank of India. RBI fixation of interest rates was always below the market rate. On account of these reasons expenditure was mounting, and public sector banks werein doldrums. Opening of the economy, liberalization, privatization, deregulation and globalization have virtually led to creation of a global village where in banking companies, for their survival, need to focus on cost, speed and quality of service to face intense competition and enormous challenges. Banks today operate under thin spreads, declining margins and rising cost. As a result of liberalization the cut-throat competition among players has emerged. Winners are those who have out-performed others, while loser are those who failed in maintaining the momentum required to sustain their position. Now banks have to perform better than other to keep ahead of the race there is need to better their own performance levels, lest they are likely to be left far behind. Public sector banks have also prepared themselves to face competition from private sector domestic and foreign banks in the areas of customer services, cost of funds, technological innovations, internal controls, motivation of staff and risk and assets management. The RBI has strengthened its supervisory machinery and at the same time ensured that enough freedom is given to banks to operate within the prescribed rules and regulations. The chief merit of the reform process was claimed to be cautious sequencing of reforms and consistent and mutually reinforcing character of the various measures taken. Introduction of prudential norms, widening of the capital base and strengthening of the organizational infrastructure have all gone hand in hand. It was noted that there had been improvement in several of the quantitative indices but there were many areas in which weaknesses still persisted. These included customer services, technological-up gradation, improvement in house keeping in terms of reconciliation of entries and balancing of books. It was further noted that the approach to handle the problem of non-performing assets differed from the recommendations. In the wake of liberalization one cannot hope to survive in isolation. Indian banking system is quite matured today. Impact of the process of reforms on the banking sector can be stated as under:

22

1. Impact of liberalization on performance of banks:

The rate of growth of deposits for public sector banks in the reforms period has come down from those prevailing in the pre-reforms period. The deposit growth rates of foreign banks declined but of domestic private banks increased. One of the main reasons behind the overall sluggish growth rate of bank deposits in the reforms period is the growth of non-bank financial intermediaries including mutual funds, finance companies and stock market. The growth rate of advances of public sector banks declined but that of private sector banks increased.

The better performance of private sector banks in the advance market is linked to their ability to attract some of the corporate clients of the public sector banks by providing them better service and better packages. PSBs have continued to occupy a predominant position in the Indian banking scene. PSBs accounted for about 72.92 per cent of the total assets of all Scheduled Commercial Banks (SCBs) as at the end of March 2003. It is, however, important to note that there has been a steady decline in the share of PSBs in the total assets of SCBs in the recent past. While PSBs accounted for 84.5 per cent of the total assets of SCBs as at the end of 1996, their share declined to 81.7 per cent in 1998 and further to 81.0 per cent in 1999 and further to 72.92 per cent in 2003.

Deterioration was observed both in the case of the SBI group as well as in the category of nationalized banks. Between end-March 1996 and end-March 2000, the SBI group lost its share by about 0.9 per cent point, while other PSBs, in the aggregate, suffered a net reduction of 3.3 per cent points during the same period.

It is important to recognize that there was enormous divergence in the performance of individual banks. Among the 27 PSBs, 7 banks improved their share, while 2 banks more or less managed to retain their share at the levels as at the end of March 1996. The SBI witnessed a decline in its share from 24.1 per cent in 1996 to 23.6 per cent in 2000. However after 2000 improvement was shown by SBI.

2. Reduction in SLR and CRR:

As recommended by the Narsimham Committee I and II, the government has reduced the SLR and CRR to a very large extent. RBI enjoys the flexibility to use CRR as an instrument of monetary policy.

3. Non-interest income of banks:

Non-interest income of banks comes from different service based activities such as credit card transactions, merchant banking, leasing etc. Before reforms, foreign banks have the highest proportion of non-interest income to their total income. However since reforms the proportion of non-interest income out of the total income of public sector banks and domestic banks has also increased. On the other hand share of non-interest income in case of foreign banks has declined from. The trends in non-interest income indicate that the domestic banks are diversifying away from their core business and have started providing increased competition to the foreign banks in the provision of fee-based services.

4. Profitability:

In the post-reform period, all the banks showed a setback as far as their profitability is concerned. In 1995-96, the majority of nationalized banks reported net losses. However in 1997-98, all the banking groups showed increase in profitability. PSBs have started witnessing an increase in profitability, particularly after the year 2000.

5. Availability of Credit:

Availability of Credit as a proportion of the total deposits of the banking sector is indicated by the credit-deposit ratios. Following the reforms the credit deposit ratio (CDR) of commercial banks as a whole declined substantially. It is partly because of the recession over the period and partly because of the banks was learning to adjust to the new lending norms under the reforms. The decrease in CDR since the reforms has been accompanied by corresponding increase in the proportion of risk-free Government securities in bank's major earning assets *i.e.* loans and advances and investments. In other words during post-reform period, the banks are investing more in government securities compared to advancing in the form of loans.

There has been an appreciable reduction in the provision of bank credit going to priority sector since the reforms. This has taken place in spite of the fact that priority sector requirement for the foreign bank has been increased substantially since reforms of 1992.

6.   Interest rate trends:

A major change introduced after the reform process in the working of banks was simplification of interest rate structure. From a situation where 38 different rates were prevalent by 1996, banks had come a very long way. Dr Rangarajan, then Governor of RBI asked banks to be in a state of readiness to meet possible challenges ahead. The warning from the regulatory authority was extremely timely.

The structure of deposit rates in the reforms period points to increasing attempt by RBI to liberalize the term deposit rate structure and boost the mobilization of both short- term and long-term deposits. One major question here in the context of the interest rate liberalization, is banks' ability to price the deposits, and their ability to price the loans. Such attempts by RBI have been made with a view to augment the resources of the banking system to prevent a liquidity crunch and consequent upward pressure on nominal lending rates. Now banks enjoy almost free hand to determine their rates of interest. Banks are free to prescribe their own lending rates, including PLR. Banks are free in the matter of interest rates determination on deposits and loans. Further, the concessional rates of interest on the priority sector lending have been withdrawn for the borrowers of higher credit amounts.

7.   Banks Vs. Non-Bank Intermediaries:

Since the financial sector reforms started in India, commercial banks have been facing increasing competition from term lending institutions like Industrial Development Bank of India (IDBI), Industrial Credit and Investment Corporation of India (ICICI), Mutual Funds, Chit Funds and the Capital market. Such competition was practically absent until recent years owing to various RBI and Government of India regulation which favoured banks in the mobilization of deposits by regulating private sector entry into financial services and due to an underdeveloped capital market. With the financial sector reforms, non-bank financial intermediaries and the capital market have experienced impressive growth in recent years. Such growth greatly increased the confidence of the small investor in non-bank deposits and investments. The share of non-bank deposits in the household savings increased and that of banks decreased. The share of bank in project loans to private sector has also declined. This was primarily due to the growth of development banks and capital market.

8. Competition:

The Indian banking industry lacked a competitive environment which affected its efficiency. To induce competitiveness in this sector, the industry was opened for the participation of private sector banks and foreign sector banks. The foreign banks were also permitted to set up shop in India either as branches or as subsidiaries. Due to these lowered entry barriers many new players entered the market.

As a result of competition, there has been a change in the market share of public and private sector banks. Any changes in favour of private and foreign banks signal the extent to which these banks have been successful by offering low prizes and better services. The market share of public sector banks in both the deposits and advances have fallen while those of private sector banks have improved. Non-bank concentration ratio gives the total market share of the largest banks in the industry. It is used to measure the extent of competition in a market. It also shows a decline in the post-reforms periods. It is due to the slower growth of the largest banks, all of which are in public sector. It is also due to increased competition from private sector banks.

9. Increased Computerization:

In the wake of liberalization, PSBs have computerized themselves right from day one. And this is not merely back-office computerization to improve house keeping but full branch automation, complete with ATMs, offering any time banking service 24 hours a day, 365 days a year. PSBs have started providing improved and faster banking services, similar to those provided by private sector and foreign banks. Greater emphasis is also now being paid on value added services such as credit cards and merchant banking. Now banks have been setting up ATMs introducing tele-banking, providing specialized services and introducing credit card operations.

10. Changed Approach of Banks:

Now banks have developed their own risk assessment models in order to price their products. Now banks have started identifying various risks and started pricing their loans accordingly.

11. Customer has become the king:

After the reforms, customer has become the king in the field of banking also. Now banks have started making concerted efforts to live upto the expectations of customers.

13.   Abolition of Branch Licensing:

After liberalisation banks are now free to start new branches keeping in mind the commercial viability of the new branches. Banks have to satisfy capital adequacy norms only to open new branch. A bank can also close its unviable branch. Branch licensing has been abolished and branch expansion norms have been relaxed enabling the banks to revamp their organizational structure. Regulations relating to the selective credit control on speculative holding of sensitive commodities were relaxed.

13.   Banks entry into Capital Market:

After liberalization banks have been allowed to raise capital from the public up to 49 per cent of the capital. This ratio has been further reduced. Various banks have taken the benefit of this opportunity to go to the capital market to raise funds. More recently, even UCO Bank and Vijay Bank have also availed this golden opportunity.

14.   Setting up of BFS and Special Debt Recovery Tribunals:

A Board of Financial Supervision has been set up to supervise banks, financial institutions and NBFCs. Various special debt recovery tribunals have also been set up in order to make quick realization.

15.   Non-Performing Assets:

Earlier the banking sector was suffering from the problem of NPAs but now concerted efforts have been made to bring down the level of NPAs particularly in public sector banks. It is very encouraging to note that there has been a substantial reduction in the level of NPAs of PSBs in the recent past.

16.   Prudential Accounting Norms:

Prudential accounting norms regarding asset classification, provisioning and income recognition have been implemented. In Indian scenario these norms are closer to international standards. The new found freedom brings in its wake new responsibilities including a measurable accountability to reflect on the quality of management. Prudential regulation relies on direct methods of:

1.   Capital adequacy.
2.   Risk weightage for assets.
3.   Different yardsticks, even degree of supervision for weak and strong banks.
4.   Accurate and timely submission of data.[4]

The introduction of prudential norms to strengthen the banks balance sheet and enhance transparency is considered as milestone measure in the financial sector reforms. These prudential norms which relate to income recognition, asset classification, provisioning for bad and doubtful debts and capital adequacy are useful in many ways--firstly, the income recognition norms reflect a true picture of the income and expenditure of the bank and secondly, the asset classification and provisioning norms help in assessing the quality of asset portfolio of the bank and finally, the capital adequacy which is based on the classification of assets suggests whether the bank is in a viable position to meet any adverse situations due a decline in the quality of its assets, or not.

Rigorous guidelines have been issued for identification of non-performing assets and for the classification of assets and there is no room for subjectivity. This was supported by capitalization of the PSBs so that over the given time frame, they comply with the norms and yet they survive to march towards future. These norms have been tightened gradually. Provisioning is required to be made for the advances which are non-performing and performing as well.

For assessing the capital adequacy ratio, weights are assigned to asset portfolio of the banks based on their riskiness. Based on the Narasimham Committee Report - I, except for cash and bank balances SLR investments all other assets were assigned risk weights. However, with the committee's second report, came the guidelines for assigning risk weights to the Government/approved securities also.

Based on the risk weighted assets of the banks, the prudential norms also prescribe the minimal capital to be maintained. Initially, the international standard of 8 per cent capital adequacy as laid by Basle Committee was accepted. However, a capital adequacy of 9 per cent was required to be maintained by the Indian banks with effect from 31 March 2000. In phases it was decided to increase it up to 10 per cent. The high standards are expected to strengthen the financial soundness of the banks, while continuing to keep them in line with international standards.

17. Valuation of Investments:
Valuation of banks investments in government securities is now done in an impartial way. In fact, these rules are at par with international practices.

Recent Trends in Indian Banking

Before liberalization, the Indian banking structure was largely controlled and parameters like branch size and location were given paramount importance. The Indian banking industry has come from a long way from being a sleepy business institution to a highly proactive and dynamic entity. The poor performance of the state owned banking institutions were due to governmental incapacity, economic inefficiency and social incomprehension. Therefore, some sort of liberal measures were needed.

Now, the Indian banking industry is going through a period of intense change, where global trends are affecting the banking business by way of increasing competition, liberalization, rising customer expectations and shrinking spreads. This transformation has been largely brought about by the large dose of liberalization and economic reforms. The importance of primary capital markets in the mid-1990, threatened banks with disintermediation and the rise of non-banking finance companies threaten them in the business of deposit mobilization itself. The focus of public attention has mostly been on the banking sector's ability to meet these challenges. New entrants are able to take advantage of the benefits of latest technology and adopt business models to leapfrog ahead. Increasing inroads from non-traditional players are being witnessed. The intense competitive retain environment forcing banks to increasing become customer-centric. Banks are embracing technology to improve customer service; design flexible and customized products increase sales opportunities and differentiate themselves in a market where product features are easily cloned. All economically developed countries are having a well knit and strong financial infrastructure. Banking development leads to economical development. Today, we are having a fairly well - developed bank system with different classes of banks-public sector banks, private sector banks - both old and new generation, foreign banks regional rural banks and cooperative banks with the RBI as the head of the system. Aside from the quantitative coverage of the banking facilities, there has been diversion of credit facilities to the hitherto neglected areas like small scale industrial sector, agricultural and other preferred areas like export sector etc. however, with the passage of time certain inadequacies developed in the quality customer service with reduced profitability, rigidity in operational areas and certain sought of permissiveness in the working culture of the banks. Unfortunately, banks in public ownership are given relatively more preferential treatment as compared to those in private sector, so a situation has emerged where some are equal and some are more equal than others. Only when there is equal opportunity to all the players, the efficiency will come to the forefront. All considered, banking system in India has come off age due to the untiring efforts of the central banking authority strong and sound banking financial architecture. The Indian economy that was a highly regulated and controlled economy is now a deregulated economy will market forces to a major extent governing the economic scene. Public sector banks are characterized by mammoth branch network, huge workforce, relatively lesser mechanization, huge volume but of less value business transactions, social objectives and their own legacy systems and procedures. Most of the public sector banks and old generation private sector banks have been taking pride in improving there volume of business, while others in the industry namely the foreign banks and new generation private sector banks consider the profit as the end product and all other things as by-products only. The public sector banks and old private sector banks go by the periodical wage settlement with the workmen. There is hierarchical multiple designations and the job is normally done on dual checking basis. During the nationalization era, banks were required to ensure economic growth by increasing the volume of credit extended especially, to various neglected sectors. Profitability and competition took a back seat in this setup of the industry. On the contrary, after liberalization, banks have to ensure profitability and that too in a highly competitive environment. Thus, the former aimed at regulated economic growth, the latter advocated market determined economic growth. Banking is a service-oriented business requiring high levels of professional and personal skills and, after globalization and liberalization; national boundaries are no longer relevant in mobilization and allocation of the capital. Now the role of banking in the process of financial intermediation has been undergoing a profound transformation, owing to changes in the global financial system. Some of the public sector banking majors are also currently in the process of finalizing their branch restructuring and staff re-deployment programmes. Since 1991, there has been a profound change in the Indian banking sector in the form of introduction of new players (foreign as well as domestic private players) and instruments, easing of controls on interest rates and their realignment with market rates, gradual reduction in resource preemption by the government, relaxation of stipulations on concessional lending and removal of concessional resource window for financial institutions. A distinction between commercial banks as providers of working capital finance and financial institutions as lenders of term finance has disappeared and both types of intermediaries have responded to the change by developing competitive packages of financial services covering long-term project financing, short-term working capital loans along with asset based financing, equipment leasing and fee based services. There has been a substantial consolidation of regulation and supervision. Banks have gradually moved to internationally acceptable norms for income recognition, asset classification and provisioning and capital adequacy. The major changes that the new economic policy sorts to introduce in the banking sector are primarily the result of the recognition that the reforms in the real sector need to be accompanied by concomitant reforms in the financial sector. If the economy has to open up to global competition, the financial sector will have to offer services that measure up to global standards.

As the economy opens up and Indian trade, commerce and industry get increasingly exposed to global competition, they would need the support of an enabling banking system, of world class standard which is available to the international competitors. In keeping with the spirit of reforms, the Monetary and Regularity authorities of the country have been removing the many shackles which had kept the Indian banking system within the narrow confines of a sheltered environment. With the gradual removal of the barriers, the banking system is now almost free to decide on a host of key areas including interest rates (both deposits and advances) credit assessment and credit dispersation, range of forex operations and so on.

Major Events in the Indian Banking Sector

The economic liberalization measures introduced by the Indian government coupled with trends towards globalization have substantially altered the banking sector and the profitability of public sector banks has declined to a large extent. So PSBs will have to introduce new financial instruments and innovations in order to remain in business. Now banks cannot function with the objective of meeting specific competition form a competitor in a market for a product. It will have to be successful in a market driven, extremely competitive, deregulated environment on a sustainable basis, so as to attract new shareholders, build loyal customer basis, attract and retain high quality staff.

The ability of banks to face competition will depend on their determined efforts at technological upgradation and improvement in operational and managerial efficiency, improvement in customer service, internal control, house- keeping and augmenting productivity and profitability. Extensive liberalization, determined stabilization and growth are vital for improving the financial sector. There is a close link between liberalization and growth. Across the world, the countries that liberalize rapidly and extensively turn around more quickly. However, this would result from committed policy measures, long-term planning, integrated approach and lack of political interference.

There is a virtual revolution in the market for financial services today with the banking sector being supplemented by the financial services industry. This has been brought about on the demand side by the need for liquid, readily transferable asset to affect transactions and on the supply side the technological changes world-wide including electronic banking and electronic funds transfer. In today's competitive era, banks need to have a strategy backed by management and organization and supported by skilled committed personnel. Under the competitive environment, the focus is on profitability and trim balance sheets. Hence, banks will need to increase fee business, concentrating on areas like guarantees, safe deposit lockers, investment advisory services, drafts and remittances.

The forces of deregulation, technology and growing customer sophistication are broadly likely to have an impact in India. But Indian bankers can eventually expect to face an environment marked by growing competition, pressure on margins and increased risks. Indian banks do not show the characteristics of efficient competitors in the banking markets, the better managed institutions will soon be making significantly progress in this sector. In the wake of liberalization banks will also have to pay great attention to strategic management, strategic planning and to greater specialization in the technical aspects of lending and credit evaluation. In order to identify appropriate competitive strategies, PSBs will have to make a careful study of the market and segment customers into various categories based on their expectations, the extent of competition, customer profitability etc.

Recommendations

On the basis of the study the following recommendations are given to the PSBs to improve their profitability and raise their productivity:

1. PSBs should strengthen their project appraisal capabilities by creating special cells, which should be manned by officers of experience, qualifications and aptitude.

2. PSBs should try to establish strategic alliances with suitable overseas banking institutions.

3. Commercial banks should be allowed to compete with financial institutions in extending term credit in clear manner.

4. PSBs should exercise some control over the volume and mix of credit portfolio within the limits of acquisition and deployment of funds.

5. PSBs should gear up their appraisal systems, monitoring mechanism and follow up reports, their by ensuring better response from the defaulters.

6. PSBs should concentrate on intensive mobilization of deposits, it can be done only through improved customer services and by implementing a various attractive deposit mobilization schemes.

7. PSBs should bring operational efficiency and should diversify their activities into non- traditional banking activities. They should concentrate on non-interest income avenues. Diversification based on niches and core competences are more likely to be successful. The strategy of offering the right kinds of product in the right market for products rather than providing everything everywhere is important to achieve a competitive advantage.

8. PSBs should find the Break Even Point of rural branches and should try to achieve the same.

9. Financial analysis, study of break even volumes of business and profitability analysis of he bank as a whole, regionwise and productwise should be made thoroughly.

10. PSBs should try to restructure their organizational functioning.

11. PSBs should move from deposit orientation to profit orientation.

12. In order to attract more and more customers, PSBs should become market savvy, but the cost of deposits and deployment plans should be kept in mind.

13. In order to raise productivity and profitability PSBs should spell turnover strategies, income- oriented and cost-oriented strategies from time to time.

14. PSBs should try to broad base the treasury functions to more centres in view of the growth of the financial sector.

15. Now PSBs have started raising money from the capital market, so they should develop and integrate a formal shareholder value analysis in their planning process.

16. Staffing and working patterns have to be reexamined from cost control point of view.

17. Banks should develop the spirit of cost consciousness among its employees. It will also help in increasing the earnings.

18. Better management information system, credit monitoring and cash management can result increase in productivity.

19. In PSBs, low compensation is the biggest demotivator for the efficient employees. So it is suggested that the pay should be linked to individual performance, group performance and overall business result of the bank. Such a pay structure will motivate the employees.

20. Committed staff especially in skill-oriented areas should be employed even by paying more, it will lead to higher productivity.

21. Better coordination with the unions may give productivity, if the unions take a positive in matters relating to transfer, placement and technology upgradation.

22. In Indian PSBs there is no clear cut placement and succession planning so in order to raise the productivity a well-defined succession plan will lead to smooth take over of important positions and it will result in a higher productivity.

23. Banks should evolve strategies for handling the recovery of NPAs and they should also improve their asset quality. It is suggested that some major legal enactments should also be made in this regard.

24. Banks should adopt scientific product pricing methods, effective asset liability management and risk management methods in order to raise their efficiency.

25. PSBs should be given autonomy to manage their affairs. They should be free to recruit and promote staff and decide the type of personnel to choose for their needs even by paying more pay packages.

26. PSBs should give comprehensive interpretation to innovative banking.

27. PSBs should evolve effective cost standards. It will help them to reduce cost and, thus, raise earning.

28. Timely SWOT analysis should be made. It will help the PSBs in improving their efficiency.

In the PSBs decentralization of financial authority is needed. A change in the attitude of the bank babus should be affected to raise the productivity and profitability.

Major Events in the Indian Banking Sector

- Report of the Narsimham Committee on Financial Sector Reform, and Introduction of new formats for annual accounts of the bank.
- Introduction of rupee convertibility on current account. Announcement of norms for floating new private sector banks.
- Establishment of State Trading Corporation of India. Introduction of FCNR (B) deposit scheme
- SBI becomes first PSB to issue shares in the capital market.
- Introduction of: Risk weighted capital adequacy norms
- Prudential norms for:
  1. Asset Classification,
  2. Income Recognition, and
  3. Provisioning for banks.

- Valuation of investment in government securities on the basis of market prices.
- Constitution of debt recovery tribunals.
- Merger of New Banks of India with Punjab National Bank.
- Reduction in the number of prescribed lending rates from six to three.
- Introduction of 365 days treasury bills with the market related rates.
- Aligning the rates of interest on dated securities of the Government with the market rates.
- Freeing of the rates of interest on deposits subject to a ceiling.
- Deregulation of interest rates on loans over Rs.2 lakh.
- Freedom to banks to decide their Prime Lending Rates (PLR) and to link loan rates to their PLR.
- Permission to the nationalized banks to raise capital up to 49 per cent of equity from capital market.
- Setting up of the Board for Financial Supervision (BFS).
- Amendment to the State Bank of India Act to allow the bank to access equity market.
- Reduction in the number of interest rates on advances from 4 to 3 and lowering of the floor lending and deposit rates.
- Budget provision of Rs. 5,700 crore to re-capitalized banks to enable them to meet new provisioning norms.

- Prescription of prudential norms for maximum non-performing assets.
- Establishment of Debt Recovery Tribunals. Introduction of the banking Ombudsman Scheme.
- Stream lining of the cash credit system
- Freedom to banks to decide their Prime Lending Rates (PLRs).
- Abolishment of Minimum Lending Rate on loan above Rs. 2 lakh.
- Conclusion of the agreement between the Government of India and the Reserve Bank of India on *ad hoc* Treasury Bills.
- Implementation of measures to strengthen secondary market in Government securities.
- Permission to the banks to purchase bonds of the Public Sector Units in the secondary market.
- Introduction of the concept of Local Area Banks.
- The State Bank of India (SBI) issued Global Depositary Receipt (GDR) and became the first Indian bank to be listed overseas.
- Six firms, promoted by banks and financial institutions, were granted licence to operate as Primary Dealers (PDs) in the Government Security market.
- Operationalization of the first shared payment network system.
- Granting of conditional autonomy to the public sector banks.
- Constitution of the board for bank frauds.
- Announcement of norms for setting up Local Area Banks. CRR was cut from 13 to 10 per cent.
- Banks cut PLR.
- Report of the Narsimham Committee on Banking Sector Reforms.
- Revision of capital adequacy norms.
- Deregulation of interest rates on term deposits.
- Deregulation of the rates on interest on foreign currency deposits to "not more than LIBOR" rates.
- Relaxation in fixed interest rate regime.

- Amendment to the Reserve Bank of India Act empowering it to supervise Non-Banking Financial Companies.
- Issuance of guidelines on asset liability management.
- Tightening of the provisioning norms for government securities and state government guaranteed loans.
- Assignment of risk weights to the government securities, state government granted loans and foreign exchange open position.
- Introduction of Kisan Credit Cards.
- Permission to banks to operate different PLRs for different maturities of loans.
- Merger of the Times Bank and HDFC bank.
- Listing of the ICICI Bank and ICICI on the New York Stock Exchange after the issue of their respective ADRs.
- Announcement of the decision of the Government to reduce its equity holding in PSBs to 33 per cent without losing their Public Sector Character.
- Advice to the banks to formulate risk management policies and to create operational set up for this task.
- Amendment to the Banking Companies (Acquisition and Transfer) Acts to allow the nationalized banks to enter insurance sector.
- Introduction of VRS in the Public Sector Banks; about 11 per cent bank employees avail the opportunity.
- The Reserve Bank of India's permission to the non-banking financial companies to convert themselves into banks.
- Large industrial houses were not allowed to start banks; they were also not allowed to hold more than 10 per cent of total equity in a bank.
- The Bank of Madura merged with the ICICI Bank.
- The RBI cut bank rate CRR to combat slow down.
- Modern bankruptcy provisions were included in the Companies Act.
- The Sick Industries Companies Act was repealed.
- The Board for Industrial Finance and Reconstruction was dissolved.
- Legislative measures were initiative to reduce the share holding of the Government on the nationalized banks to 33 per cent.

- The RBI announced revised norms of establishing new banks in the private sector.
- The banks and NBFCs were permitted to undertake insurance business.
- The RBI announced the transaction to a full-fledged Liquidity Adjustment Facility.
- The norms of banks' exposure to the capital market were relaxed.
- Measures to improve credit delivery system were announced.
- The Government announced its resolve to enable the banks to affect speedier recovery of funds locked up
- in NPAs.
- Minimum maturity period for certificate of deposits was reduced from three months to 15 days.
- Norms for the issue of commercial papers were made more flexible.
- A system of consolidated reported including the accounts of the subsidiaries was introduced.
- The State Bank of India raised rupees 25,612 crore under the Indian Millennium Deposit (IMD) from the NonResident Indians.
- A proposal for the close monitoring for suit filed and decreed accounts on an ongoing basis was initiated.
- It was decided that the concept of capital funds in India as defined under capital adequacy standards for determining exposure ceiling uniformly would be implemented from March 31, 2002.
- Guidelines were issued for compromise settlement of dues of banks through Lok Adalats. Banks were advised that all cases of wilful defaults of Rs.1 crore and above should be reviewed and suits filed, if not done earlier.
- Banks wee advised to provide a personal insurance package to all Kisan Credit Cards (KCCs) holders to cover them against accident death or permanent disability up to a maximum of Rs. 50,000 and Rs. 25,000 respectively.
- PSBs were advised to earmark 5 per cent of their net bank credit for lending to women and the target is required to be achieved by March 31, 2004.

- It was decided to permit banks on an experimental basis, to extend finance to stockbrokers for margin trading within the overall ceiling of 5 per cent prescribed for exposure of banks to capital marke, subject to certain conditions. It was indicated that these guidelines, valid for a period of 60 days, up to November 22, 2001 would be reviewed in the light of actual experience.
- Banks were advised to furnish in their Balance Sheets the disclosures regarding movement of provisions held towards NPAs and movement of provisions held towards depreciation on investments.
- Consolidated guidelines were issued on Foreign Direct Investment (FDI) in the banking sector.
- The RBI advised that while reckoning the period of quantum of unsecured advances and guarantees for applying the norms relating to unsecured advances and guarantee, outstanding credit card dues should be excluded from the total of unsecured advances.
- All PSBs were advised that they may, on the basis of good track record of the SSI units and the financial position of the units, increase the limit of dispensation of collateral requirement from Rs.5 lakh to Rs.15 lakh.
- Banks were permitted to invest their FCNR(B) deposits in longer term fixed income instruments with appropriate rating prescribed for the money market instruments, with prior approval of their Boards regarding the type, tenure, rating and likely cap on such investments within the ALM guidelines in force.
- Banks were advised that w.e.f. March 31, 2005, an asset would be classified as doubtful if it remained in the sub-standard category for 12 months. Banks were allowed to phase the additional provisioning consequent upon the reduction in the transition period from substandard to doubtful assess from 18 months to 12 months over a 4 year period, commencing from the year ending march 31, 2005, with a minimum of 20 per cent each year.
- Banks were advised to compute Investment Fluctuation Reserve (IFR) with reference to investments in two categories, *i.e.* Held for Trading and Available for Sale and not include investments underheld to maturity for the purpose.

- Compliance with AS-17, AS-18, AS-21 and AS-22 was made optional for the banks only for the year ended March 31, 2002. Banks would be required to conform to these ASs by March 31, 2003 in accordance with the detailed guidelines awaited from the Working Group on the issue.
- Banks were advised to submit the list of suit filed accounts of Rs.1 crore and above as on March 31, 2002 and quarterly updates thereof till December 2002 and suit filed accounts for wilful defaulters of Rs.25 lakh and above as at end March, June, September and December 2002, to the RBI and to Credit Information Bureau (India) Limited (CIBIL) for a period of one year till March 31, 2003 and thereafter to CIBIL only.
- The winds of liberalisation have totally changed the banking industry resulting in the generation of intensely competitive environment. The banking areas have been almost completely flooded with new entrants including private banks, foreign banks, non-banking finance companies (NBFCs), the merchant bankers and chit funds etc.
- The Indian banking system has witnessed a significant transformation in recent years. Indian banks, before the institution of financial sector reforms, operated in a highly regulated environment with regard to different parameters, such as branch location, deposit and lending rates and deployment of credit, to mention a few. Further in view of the social responsibility placed on the banking sector, profitability was not considered as an important yardstick of their performance. The main thrust of banking operations was on social banking by enlarge banking remained concentrated on public sectored and functioned in highly regulated environment. With the institutions of financial sector reforms, competition among the banks has increased.

Factors Affecting the Relative Share of Banks

There are a number of factors which affect the relative share of Banks. These are:

1. **Share of rural branches:**

The share of deposits of branches in rural and semi-urban areas in the case of PSBs has been very high. In India, SBI has the highest percentage of rural branches. Foreign banks did not have any branch in the rural areas.

2. Average branch size:

Banks which are relatively large may be in a position to reap certain scale economies. The relationship between size and performance would depend upon the net outcome of these two counteracting influences. The size can be evaluated in different ways. As deposits form an important item under liability, the size of the banks in terms of deposits could be regarded as a proxy to indicate size. While the size of the bank in terms of the total deposit is important, the average size of the branch can be considered as a more important indicator.

3. Profit performance:

Trends in various profit indicators in the case of public sector banks shows that these banks recorded a significant improvement in the profit performance over the last five years. It needs to be noted that during the year 1999-2000. there was a sharp improvement in the profitability in case of all banks.

Share of priority sector advances:

In the case of public sector banks, the share of priority sector lending stood at 37.8 per cent of the net bank credit in March 1996 to 43.6 per cent of the net bank credit in March 2000.

Public Sector Banks dominate the market and account for the major share of deposits, advances and branches. As the Indian banking sector restructures there will be casualties - some painful -but it is difficult to believe that a country with such high level of education, work ethic and proven entrepreneurial flair that are demonstrated by the Indians both domestically and abroad will not be a fertile soil for several outstanding banks. Building a significant and sustainable presence in a foreign banking market is a difficult, expensive and highly risky understanding. Several UK banks have lost large amount of money in attempting to penetrate the US market, many US banks have had their finger burnt in Europe. Within Indian domestic banks - for all their problems - hold several trump cards, including an unrivalled knowledge of the market, deep-rooted relationships and a potentially unmatched capability to assess, price and manage credit risks. Banks are also restructuring and consolidating to meet the challenge of managing vast cross-border flows. As banks the world over recover and reorient their activities in deregulated financial markets, there is greater concern for improved risk management and capital adequacy. To meet the challenge of globalization, banks are concentrating on being efficient, specializing in key areas of strength, innovating products and in general becoming more responsive to customer's requirements. They are also doing away with those areas which other can do more efficiently, establishing strategic alliances and interacting through globalization. They have been trying to increase their earnings from non-lending activities including trading and advisory services, risk management, insurance etc.

As international trade increases, flow of finance directly associated with trade also increases. As financial markets become broader and deeper, it gives importers and exporters better access to finance and innovation steps in to make international finance expand. There has, thus, been an increase in the volume of cross-border financial with the focus on competition, efficiency and coordination in supervision.

Challenges Ahead
The banking system in India faces a threat from several fronts. Liberalization is leading to a restructuring of Indian industry and banks need to manage the restructuring to ensure that there asset quality does not deteriorate any further technological change in the shape of Internet threatened to move the bank's best customer to those banks who were the first to get on the Net. The internet reduced entry barriers to banking and resulting in more competition. The attraction of other financial products such as mutual funds steadily increased. Financial institutions, banks, credit card companies and consumer finance companies have increasingly tread on each others toes.

Our banking system, however, faces several difficult challenges. Some of the challenges are external for example the phenomenal growth in the volume of capital flows across nations and the consequent integration of financial markets across the globe.

Unlike ten or 20 years ago, Indian banks can no longer be isolated from international developments and international capital movements. These developments have brought with them both immense benefits as well as costs.[6]

There are a number of areas where cooperation will be required not only for efficiency but also to ensure that market forces work properly. Some of these are:

1. Development of technological infrastructure.
2. Organization and management of markets.
3. A distinct relationship between producers and distributors of products and services.

After viewing prevailing winds in the Indian financial system and the markets, it becomes evident that there is a compelling need to rethink the strategies, to refashion these strategies and to decide what should be done next.

Conclusion

The Indian banking sector has witnessed a remarkable shift in its operational environment during the last decade. Various reform measures both qualitative and quantitative were introduced with an objective to revitalize the banking sector and enable it to meet the future challenges. The reform process undertaken by the government has been implemented in a phased manner to allow the banks to have a level playing field and to tune themselves with the changes. Liberalisation of the sector has resulted in the advent of new generation banks in the private sector which have redefined the service spectrum of the banks. Profit maximization has always been subject to constraint of acceptable level of risk. In a nutshell, it may be concluded that globalization has made the existing institutional arrangement of the banking sector deficient in many ways. The major issues related to international competitiveness consists of financial soundness, operational efficiency, commercial viability and profitability. There has been a change in the perception of the government and RBI both. The government has raised the borrowing rates to make them competitive and realistic. The RBI has rationalized its organization by adding one more board to supervise the banks. The lending rates have been simplified. SLR and CRR reduced and the accounting practices have been changed. Restriction on expansion and entry of new private sector banks has been relaxed. Nevertheless, much is desired for a systemic approach to deal with endogenous and long-term problems so that the banking sector ushers into the era of prosperity and compete with multinational institutions.

CHAPTER – III
PRODUCTIVITY ANALYSIS

Productivity Analysis

Productivity is a vital indicator of economic performance of an economic system. Productivity is not an end in itself. In fact, it is a mechanism for improving the material quality of life. Productivity is fundamental to progress throughout the world. It is at the heart of economic growth and development, improvements in standards of living and quality of life.

Definition

Productivity is defined as the goods and services produced per unit of labour, capital or both. The ratio of output to labour and capital is a total productivity measure. In simple words, productivity is the output per unit of input employed.

Kopleman has defined productivity as the relationship between physical output of one or more of the associated physical inputs used in production. When single input is used to measure productivity, it is called 'factor productivity' and when all factors are combined together for the purpose, it is known as 'total factor productivity.

Concept of Productivity in Banking

The concept and definition of productivity as applied in manufacturing industries cannot be applied as such in banking industry because it is primarily a service industry. In the field of banking, the various products are accounts, drafts, exchange remittances, cheques, travellers cheques, credit cards, debit cards, services for guarantees, various kinds of loans like housing loan, education loan, car loan etc. Identification and measurement of output in banking is very difficult exercise as it is not possible to bring various services to measure output. However, banking being an important economic activity cannot afford to loose sight of the concept of productivity. Application of the concept in the Indian banking industry becomes all the more difficult, as it gets associated with such diverse aspects like operational cost effectiveness, profitability, customer services, priority sector lending, mobilization of deposits, deployment of credit in rural and backward regions. But as we know that banks are the mirror of an economy. Therefore better functioning of banking sector may lead to the overall improvement of the economy. In fact, banks act as a link between those who want to save and those who want to invest, so improvement in the productivity of the banking sector is very much needed who want to save and obviously, difficulty is not in applying the broader concept of productivity as ratio of output and input, but is in measuring output in the form of services. The concept of productivity analysis in banking sector may give misleading results, if not used carefully. If we see the productivity of PSBs in relation to the productivity of foreign banks, then it will be noticed that productivity of foreign banks (say business per employee) is much higher, but such comprise is misleading. Productivity at the national level is dependent on various factors like per capita income, saving habits and banking habits. In addition to it, there are regional variations which affect the productivity of various players in the banking field. So in order to have a reliable idea of productivity, it is necessary to analyze every segment, different sizes of banks and regionwise positioning of banks.

As in banking industry in India, volume of business became progressively imperative to secure more resources for meeting social objectives while maintaining viability of operations, business level may be preferred as being more representative of productivity.[2]

Productivity helps firms, industries and nations to achieve sustainable competitive advantage. Industry is a thrust area for countries in their quest for competitiveness. It must be noted that banks which have maintained the momentum of continuous growth, and profitability showed better ratio of manpower effectiveness. Each element has crucial sub- components which serve as building blocks for productivity. The Government policies effectively support competitiveness if they are structures around productivity driven reform mechanism, cost deflating tariff structure and technology and industry vision.[3]

C.B. Rao has proposed a productivity competitiveness model particularly for Indian environment. The model comprises of three elements viz.
1.   Government Policies.
2.   Industry Strategies.
3.   Management Methods.

Competitive market conditions and liberalized economic and industrial policies demand more strident attention to productivity improvement and restructuring of industries. Continuous upgradation of technical knowledge, discovery of new ways for productivity improvement and flexible redeployment of skills in new activities are vital for the competitive age. Similarly introduction of systems of employee participation such as quality circles and TQM system would be necessary to keep the employees on the leading edge of their skills and motivation.

The level of productivity orientation in various elements affects the overall level of competitiveness. The three element dynamic model of productivity and competitiveness has been shown in Figure 3.1. The Indian government has launched a liberaisation programme to dismantle controls and for shifting towards market driven economy. To have the benefits from such measures, productivity driven reform mechanism is necessary, only then the real benefit of liberalization can be enjoyed.

In India the need of the hour is substantial improvement in productivity of PSBs. Since the performance of the bank will play an important role in deciding the overall performance of the real sector, their productivity is very critical to the overall productivity of the country. Studies have clearly brought out the extent to which the below mentioned factors are responsible for low productivity in Indian banks as compared to American banks. In the study, productivity is defined as number of transactions and the number of loans and deposit accounts per hour per employee. According to the study the three reasons for the wide gap between Indian and US banks are:

• Technology (Lack of branch automation and centralized processing).
• Systematic inefficiencies.
• Scale.

Productivity of a bank can be improved by reducing the cost of disintermediation and by raising the spread that is deploying capital in the most effective way. The study has focused on how PSBs and old generation private sector banks can improve productivity by managing some of the important

Sources of Productivity
Jagwant Singh[4] has studied following main sources of productivity:

1. Changes in capital/labour ratio.
2. Improvement in technological knowledge.

3. Improvement in managerial knowledge.
4. Education.
5. Demographic changes.
6. Changes in hours of work.
7. Reallocation of resources.
8. Regulations
9. Economies of scale and increased specialization.
10. Entrepreneurship and social attitudes.
11. Irregular factors.
12. Miscellaneous determinants.

Thus, attitudinal change, adaptability and openness to new ideas, techniques and technology by executives at all levels are the first prerequisite of success of any programme, be it long range planning or a programme of productivity improvement.

Why Productivity is Low in PSBs?

Following factors are responsible for low productivity in PSBs:

1. Dual control by RBI as well as government:
The banking system suffers from the fact that it is serving two masters. Both the Finance Ministry and RBI seem to have equal say in the affairs of the bank. The government should make its expectation from the banking system very clear and leave their realization to debt handling of RBI.

2. Lack of autonomy
Lack of Aatonomy together with governmental fears like directed investment and directed credit programmes adds to the systemic inefficiencies and results in lower productivity. PSBs face excessive administrative and political interferences in internal credit decision-making and internal management.

3. Unproductive competition:
The SBI, its seven associates and the additional 20 nationalized banks, have all been allowed to retain their individual entities. Different banks even though they themselves belong to the public sector, spend considerable time competing among themselves without increasing the total benefit to the system. As a result the focus on banks has shifted away from the areas of real productivity.

It is very difficult to speculate in what manner the 27 banks should be reformed and into what precise manner? However, the best option would be to divest government holding as promised, so that the mergers between banks could be market-driven rather than a bail-out consideration.

4.   Lock up of funds in NPAs:

Non-performing assets continue to be the primary source of misery and ever present Damocles swords threatening to question the fundamental efficiencies of banks. The major shortcoming is the absence of any systematic effort to identify, train and position officials with the required proficiency to handle the credit functions.

5.   Policy of appeasement towards the union

Though, over the last couple of years, Bank Union has been lying low yet they refuse to subscribe the principles and practices of participative management and have victimized the middle and branch management sheer collective power to stop work and cause around havoc. Although the bank unions have the guaranteed right to collective on behave of the employees, they have no right to go on strike.

6.   Work culture:

Productivity is a function not always related to the size and technology only but also to various other factors like work culture, service diversification etc. It should be noticed that personnel functioning in Indian and foreign banks have different work culture. Particularly in PSBs, work culture is entirely discouraging.

7.   Deficient training systems

Another main cause of low productivity in case of Indian banks is the deficiencies in the training systems. Training modules used these days are totally irrelevant. Training system should focus on the quality of services given to the customers. Training programme should enable every individual to work as a member of an effective team and realize the potential.

Major Indicators of Productivity
1.   **Business Volume (Deposits + Advances) / No. of Employees**

This is the most common productivity indicator used by banks. This ratio does not reflect fully the wide range of services provided by the banks. The business per employee is more than six times higher in foreign banks operating in India as compared to PSBs. This comparison may be biased representation of employee productivity because of the difference between technology, process and procedures followed by foreign banks as compared to PSBs.

2. (Working Fund + Contingent Liability) / No. of Employees

This ratio represents the value of business based on bothfund and nonfund related activities. The ratio shows that foreign banks, on an average perform 30 times than PSBs. Private banks perform 10 times better than PSBs on this parameter. The largest share of this difference is due to non-fund businesses where foreign banks are very strong

3. Net Total Income/No. of Employees and Net Profit/No. of Employees

The foreign banks perform 10 times better than PSBs on net total income per employee and about 20 times better on net profit per employee. The comparison clearly reflex that foreign and private banks have much higher operational efficiency as compared to PSBs.

4. Working Fund/Establishment Cost

This ratio indicates how effectively human resources hasworked in generating business for the bank. However the private sector banks have performed better than foreign banks and PSBs on this arameter

The following ratios have been used in order to study the productivity of PSBs.

Per Employee Indicators (Labour Productivity)
1. Deposit per employee
2. Advances per employee
3. Business per employee
4. Total expenditure per employee
5. Total income per employee
6. Spread per employee
7. Net profit per employee
8. Burden per employee

Per Branch Indicators (Branch Productivity)

1. Deposits per branch
2. Advances per branch
3. Business per branch
4. Total income per branch
5. Total expenditure per branch
6. Burden per branch
7. Net profit per branch
8. Spread per branch

Employee Productivity of PSBs

Human resource is the most important asset of an organization and banking business is no exception to it. But Indian PSBs are known for their excessive staff strength, it affects their productivity. In the present study, employee productivity of PSBs has been evaluated by taking eight ratios in consideration. A brief summary of all these ratios are as under:

1. Deposits per Employee:

This ratio has been computed by dividing the amount of total deposits by the number of employees in the bank. The ratio has shown an upward trend (in absolute terms) in general as shown in Table 3.1. In 1996 the ratio was the highest in the case of BOB with Rs. 33.00 lakh per employee and the lowest in case of SBM with Rs. 17.17 lakh per employee. In 2007, OBC with Rs.209.64 lakh per employee was on the top followed by COB with Rs.184.84 lakh per employee.

2. Advances per Employee:

This ratio has been computed by dividing the amount of total advances by the number of employees in the bank. The ratio has shown an upward trend (in absolute terms) in general as shown in Table 3.2. In 1996 the ratio was the highest in the case of IB with Rs.21.90 lakh per employee and lowest in case of SBM with 9.64 lakh per employee. In 2007. UntBI with Rs.119.07 lakh per employee was on the top followed by COB with Rs.107.32 lakh per employee.

3. Total income per employee:

This ratio has been computed by dividing the amount of total income by the number of employees in the bank. The ratio has shown an upward trend (in absolute terms) in general as shown in Table 3.3. In 1996 the ratio was the highest in the case of IB with Rs. 3.91 lakh per employee and lowest

50

in case of SBM with Rs. 1.95 lakh per employee. In 2007, OBC with Rs. 25.86 lakh per employee was on the top followed by UntBI with Rs. 25.14 lakh per employee.

4.   Total expenditure per employee:

This ratio has been computed by dividing the amount of total expenditure by the number of employees in the bank. The ratio has shown an upward trend (in absolute terms) in general as shown in Table 3.4. In 1996 the ratio was the highest in the case of IB with Rs. 3.83 lakh per employee and the lowest in case of SBM with Rs. 1.92 lakh per employees.
In 2007, OBC with Rs. 22.70 lakh per employee was on the
top followed by UntBI with Rs.20.30 lakh per employee.

5.   Net profit per employee:

This ratio has been computed by dividing the amount of total amount of net profits by the number of employees in the bank. The ratio has shown an upward trend (in absolute terms) in general as shown in Table 3.5. In 1996 the ratio was the highest in the case of CB with Rs.0.15 lakh per employee and the lowest in case of UCB and VB. In 2007. OBC with Rs.2.36 lakh per employee was on the top followed by SBP with Rs.1.97 lakh per employee.

6.   Spread per employee:

This ratio has been computed by dividing the amount of total amount of spread by the number of employees in the bank. The ratio has shown an upward trend (in absolute terms) in general as shown in Table 3.6. In 1996 the ratio was the highest in the case of OBC with Rs.0.88 lakh per employee and the lowest in case of SBP with Rs.0.37 lakh per employee. In 2007, UntBI with Rs.7.44 lakh per employee was on the top followed by OBC with Rs.7.15 lakh per employee.

7.   Business per employee:

This ratio has been computed by dividing the amount of total business by the number of employees in the bank. The ratio has shown an upward trend (in absolute terms) in general as shown in Table 3.7. In 1996 the ratio was the highest in the case of BOI with Rs.54.02 lakh per employee and lowest in case of SBM with Rs.26.79 lakh per employee. In 2007, OBC with Rs.313.83 lakh per employee was on the
top followed by COB with Rs.292.16 lakh per employee.

8. Burden per employee:

This ratio has been computed by dividing the amount of total burden by the number of employees in the bank. The ratio has shown an upward trend (in absolute terms) in general as shown in Table 3.8. In 1996 the ratio was the highest in the case of OBC with Rs.0.66 lakh per employee and the lowest in case of SBP with Rs.0.25 lakh per employee. In 2007, SB with Rs.2.94 lakh per employee was on the top followed by UntBI with Rs.2.60 lakh per employee.

Branch Productivity of PSBs

While evaluating the results in terms of infrastructural facilities utilized by the banks at various locations, places, again eight indicators have been used. A brief summary of these ratios are as under:

1. Deposits per branch:

This ratio has been computed by dividing the amount of total deposits by the number of branches in the bank. The ratio has shown an upward trend (in absolute terms) in general as shown in Table 3.9. In 1996 the ratio was the highest in the case of BOI with Rs. 748.33 lakh per branch and the lowest in case of BOM with Rs.305.63 lakh per branch. In 2007. SBI with Rs.2978.10 lakh per branch was on the top followed by OBC with Rs.2946.06 lakh per branch.

2. Advances per branch:

This ratio has been computed by dividing the amount of total advances by the number of branches in the bank. The ratio has shown an upward trend (in absolute terms) in general as shown in Table 3.10. In 1996 the ratio was the highest in the case of BOI with Rs.480.84 lakh per branch and the lowest in case of DB with Rs.151.66 lakh per branch. In 2007, COB with Rs.1667.29 lakh per branch was on the top followed by UntBI with Rs.1639.82 lakh per branch.

3. Total income per branch:

This ratio has been computed by dividing the amount of total income by the number of branches in the bank. The ratio has shown an upward trend (in absolute terms) in general as shown in Table 3.11. In 1996 the ratio was the highest in the case of BOI with Rs.80.58 lakh per branch and the lowest in case of DB with Rs.33.83 lakh per branch. In 2007, SBI with Rs.374.07 lakh per branch was on the top followed by OBC with 363.43 lakh per branch.

4. Total expenditure per branch:

This ratio has been computed by dividing the amount of total expenditure by the number of branches in the bank. The ratio has shown an upward trend (in absolute terms) in general as shown in Table 3.12. In 1996 the ratio was the highest in the case of BOI with Rs.79.62 lakh per branch and the lowest in case of DB with Rs. 33.06 lakh per branch. In 2007, OBC with Rs.319.04 lakh per branch was on the top followed by SBI with Rs.307.54 lakh per branch.

5. Net profit per branch:

This ratio has been computed by dividing the amount of total NP by the number of branches in the bank. The ratio has shown an upward trend (in absolute terms) in general as shown in Table 3.13. In 1996 the ratio was the highest in the case of SBP with Rs.2.56 lakh per branch and the lowest in case of UCB. In 2007, COB with Rs.46.75lakh per branch was on the top followed by OBC with Rs.33.15 lakh per branch.

The term profit is an accounting concept which shows the excess of income over expenditure viewed during a specified period of time. Profit is the main reason for the continued existence of every commercial organization. On the other hand, the term profitability is a relative measure where profit is expressed as a ratio, generally as a percentage. Profitability depicts the relationship of the absolute amount of profit with various other factors. Profitability is a relative concept which is quite useful in decision-making. Another main issue here is profit planning, which consists of various steps to be taken to improve the profitability of the bank.

Profit is the very reason for the continued existence of every commercial organization. The rate of profitability and volume of profits are therefore, rightfully considered as indicators of efficiency in the deployment of resources of banks.[1]

Profitability indicates earning capacity of the banks. It highlights the managerial competency of the banks. It also portrays work culture, operating efficiency of the bank.

Profitability is the most important and reliable indicator as it gives a broad indication of the ability of a bank to raise its income level. Profitability of banks is affected by a number of factors. Some of these are endogenous, some are exogenous and yet structural. Changes in policies made by RBI are exogenous to the system. This includes changes in momentary policy, changes in quantitative credit control like changes in CRR, SLR, manipulation of bank rates, qualitative credit controls like selective credit control measures, C/D ratio, regionwise guidelines on lending to priority sectors, changes in interest rates on deposits and advances, levy of tax on interest income etc. Various other factors like careful control of expenditure, timely recovery of loans are endogenous. Various structural factors include geographical spread of bank branches, decentralization in the management and structural changes in deposits and advances. Banking structure and profitability structure of banking system across countries have a bearing on the profitability of banks.[3] The profitability of banks is affected one way or the other by these factors, either individually or jointly. Bank profitability is causing concern to all. After libralisation, profitability has regained its lost importance. Now efforts are being directed to achieve the profitability targets. The profitability of public sector banks has been indicating a fast declining trend in the past and the situation in future may not be different if all the concerned do not take timely preventive measures before the situation goes out of control. Since all the banks in the country function under similar environments, the low performance of any bank can be attributed to a larger extent to their managerial inefficiency and structural deficiency. Certain populistic Central Government disregarding the basic banking principles, coupled with lethargic attitude of the management of nationalized banks lead to inefficiency, in-competency and deceleration in performance.[4] The major reasons for this declining profitability can be summarized as under:

1. Non-Performing advances leading to bad debts..
2. Legal Expenses to recovers the bad debts..
3. Cut Throat competition among banks to lure deposits.
4. Narrowing Spread.
5. Branch Expansion on unviable consideration.
6. Ineffective organizational restructuring.
7. Lack of proper management of resources.
8. More concentration on deposit orientation than profit orientation.
9. Increasing burden of administrative expenses.
10. Increasing establishment expenses.
11. Ineffective marketing strategies resulting in reduction in market share.
12. No turn-over strategies.
13. Ineffective cost-oriented strategies.

14. Subsidized service charges like concession granted.
15. Ineffective environment scanning.

The problem of low profitability and designing profitability has been historical to the banking system. "The banks are virtually suffering from scissors crisis, with a declining rate of increase in earnings and rising costs.

The profitability analysis of commercial banks used to be a frustrating experience as the financial statements of banks concealed much and revealed less. But now-a-days, after liberalization under pressure from regulatory agencies and the public, the trend has changed. So now the profitability analysis of commercial banks means something. The financial statements of commercial banks are now prepared keeping in mind are the various changes, so they reveal each and every aspect.

Profits have been, and are under tremendous pressure. Declining trends in profits and profitability have become a major cause of concern for all and in order to ensure the survival and growth of this vital sector of economy, it becomes essential to identify various factors which have studiedly contributed towards the decline in bank profitability so that corrective action can be taken and future profitability is ensured. The major factors that have a bearing on the financial viability of the banks are:

1. Priority Sector Lending.
2. Credit Policies.
3. Massive Geographical Expansion.
4. Industrial Sickness.
5. Growing Competition.
6. Deposit Composition.
7. Increasing Establishment Expenses.
8. Low Income from Ancillary Business.
9. Spread and Burden - Their Backward Linkages and Movements.
10. Miscellaneous Factors (Like declining credit AND mounting overdue).

The present trend of low and declining profitability can be arrested and reversed if the remedial measures are tried in right direction to ease the pressure on profitability.

The profit rates obtained by using sales or value added as denominators will therefore give us a short-term perspective of profitability. The return on capital employed on investments or total assets or fixed assets as variously defined, on the other hand will give us long-term perspective of profitability

Summary, Conclusions and Recommendations

The present chapter summarizes the main findings of the study and puts forward suggestions on the basis of the findings of the study.

The Banking system must be on a sound footing not only to instill public confidence but also to make banks capable of discharging their social responsibility. A number of factors like the entry of the overseas financial intermediaries into domestic financial markets necessitated some kinds of charges. Banking Sector being the heart line of the financial maket, their up gradation and financial strength is more vital for an efficient financial system. With these views, RBI and government had initiated the process of banks reforms by setting up Narasimham Committee-I in 1991 and thereafter Narasimhanm Committee-II in 1998. Thus, the bank reforms heralded the beginning of implementing prudential norms consisting of capital adequacy ratio, asset classification, income recognition, and provisioning. Broadly, banking sector reforms have been concerned with improving

1. The Policy Framework

2. The Financial Health

3. The Institutional Infrastructure

In the Indian context, banking is really the mirror of economic growth of the country. Before liberalization, the Indian banking structure was largely controlled and parameters like branch size and location were given paramount importance. The Indian banking industry has come from a long way from being a sleepy business institution to a highly proactive and dynamic entity. Now, the Indian banking industry is going through a period of intense change, where global a trends are affecting the banking business increasing competition, liberalization, rising customer expectations, shrinking spreads, increasing disintermediation, competitive prizing and possibilities macro-volatility. This transformation has been largely brought about by the large dose of liberalization and economic reforms.

Liberalization

Liberalisation involves freeing prizes, trade and entry from state controls. In fact, the degree to which an economy is free can be defined by scope of state involvement, either directly by ownership or indirectly by regulation, in markets for products or services. Liberalisation does not raise real interests and results in an increased diversity of financial instruments. Unwary investors may be taken by the rather fanciful terms offered. In fact, as a result of liberalization, now there is a pressure on profits and profitability of public sector banks. It can lead to speculation and create problems of systematic failures. In fact, liberalization and deregulation encompasses the following:

1. Interest rate and other price deregulation measures.
2. Removal of direct credit controls and mandatory investment regulations.
3. Measures design to promote entry of new competitors.
4. Supportive merger and ownership policy.
5. Prudential regulation and reliance on indirect tools for controls.
6. Transparency.

Productivity

Productivity is a vital indicator of economic performance. In simple words, it is output-input ratio. It is a relationship between given output and the means used to produce it. Banking is primarily a service industry. There are number of indicators to measure the productivity of banking sector. Measures of productivity at bank or industry level may differ from the indicators of productivity at branch level.

Productivity is affected by man power, mechanization, system and the procedures, costing of operations, customer services and various external aspects.

Profitability

Profitability is a rate expressing profit as a percentage of total asset or sales or any other variable to represent the relationship. In fact, there may be various dimensions of profitability analysis. A large number of ratios can be used in order to measure the banks profitability as

1. Interest Income to Working Funds Ratio.
2. Interest Expended to Working Funds Ratio.
3. Spread to Working Funds Ratio.
4. Non-Interest Income to Working Funds Ratio.
5. Non-Interest Expenditure to Working Funds Ratio.
6. Burden to Working Funds Ratio.
7. Net Profit to Working Funds Ratio.
8. Interest Income to Total Income.
9. Interest Expended to Total Expenditure Ratio, and
10. Staff Expenditure to Total Expenditure Ratio.

Objectives of the Study

The main objectives of this study are as under:

1. To evaluate profitability and productivity of PSBs in the *viz-a-viz* post liberalization period.
2. To identify the various factors affecting he profitability and productivity of PSBs in the post-liberalization period,
3. To examine the contribution of various factors towards the profitability and productivity of PSBs in the *viz-a-viz* post-liberalization period.
4. To make suggestions for the improvement in the profitability and productivity of PSBs.
5. To create platform for future research in this area.

To conclude, it can be said that growth in business per employee, Net profit per employee and total income per employee shows moderate growth in employee productivity. As far as burden per branch is concerned, it has shown a mixed phenomenon. As far as productivity is concerned, it has shown a mixed phenomenon. As far as productivity is concerned, SBI has remained the leader in the State Bank group. It is very much clear from the result that as a result of liberalization, work culture of PSBs has improved, which has favourably affected the productivity ratios. As far as branch productivity is concerned freedom in this field have favourably affected the productivity is concerned freedom in this field have favourably affected the productivity of PSBs. On the basis of T-Scores (Overall Productivity) also, it becomes evident that BOB, BOI, SBI, COB, OBC have top rankers whereas the ranking of SBBJ, SB, AIIB, SBM and UCB was far from satisfactory

Conclusions

The economic liberalization measures introduced by the Indian government coupled with trends towards globalization have substantially altered the banking sector and the profitability of public sector banks has declined to a large extent. So PSBs will have to introduce new financial instruments and innovations in order to remain in business. Now banks cannot function with the objective of meeting specific competition form a competitor in a market for a product. It will have to be successful in a market driven, extremely competitive, deregulated environment on a sustainable basis, so as to attract new shareholders, build loyal customer basis, attract and retain high quality staff.

The ability of banks to face competition will depend on their determined efforts at technological upgradation and improvement in operational and managerial efficiency, improvement in customer service, internal control, house- keeping and augmenting productivity and profitability. Extensive liberalization, determined stabilization and growth are vital for improving the financial sector. There is a close link between liberalization and growth. Across the world, the countries that liberalize rapidly and extensively turn around more quickly. However, this would result from committed policy measures, long-term planning, integrated approach and lack of political interference.

There is a virtual revolution in the market for financial services today with the banking sector being supplemented by the financial services industry. This has been brought about on the demand side by the need for liquid, readily transferable asset to affect transactions and on the supply side the technological changes world-wide including electronic banking and electronic funds transfer. In today's competitive era, banks need to have a strategy backed by management and organization and supported by skilled committed personnel. Under the competitive environment, the focus is on profitability and trim balance sheets. Hence, banks will need to increase fee business, concentrating on areas like guarantees, safe deposit lockers, investment advisory services, drafts and remittances.

The forces of deregulation, technology and growing customer sophistication are broadly likely to have an impact in India. But Indian bankers can eventually expect to face an environment marked by growing competition, pressure on margins and increased risks. Indian banks do not show the characteristics of efficient competitors in the banking markets, the better managed institutions will soon be making significantly progress in this sector. In the wake of liberalization banks will also have to pay great attention to strategic management, strategic planning and to greater specialization in the technical aspects of lending and credit evaluation. In order to identify appropriate competitive strategies, PSBs will have to make a careful study of the market and segment customers into various categories based on their expectations, the extent of competition, customer profitability etc.

Recommendations

- On the basis of the study the following recommendations are given to the PSBs to improve their profitability and raise their productivity:
- PSBs should strengthen their project appraisal capabilities by creating special cells, which should be manned by officers of experience, qualifications and aptitude.
- PSBs should try to establish strategic alliances with suitable overseas banking institutions.
- Commercial banks should be allowed to compete with financial institutions in extending term credit in clear manner.
- PSBs should exercise some control over the volume and mix of credit portfolio within the limits of acquisition and deployment of funds.
- PSBs should gear up their appraisal systems, monitoring mechanism and follow up reports, their by ensuring better response from the defaulters.
- PSBs should concentrate on intensive mobilization of deposits, it can be done only through improved customer services and by implementing a various attractive deposit mobilization schemes.
- PSBs should bring operational efficiency and should diversify their activities into non- traditional banking activities. They should concentrate on non-interest income avenues. Diversification based on niches and core competences are more likely to be successful. The strategy of offering the right kinds of product in the right market for products rather than providing everything everywhere is important to achieve a competitive advantage.
- PSBs should find the Break Even Point of rural branches and should try to achieve the same.
- Financial analysis, study of break even volumes of business and profitability analysis of he bank as a whole, regionwise and productwise should be made thoroughly.
- PSBs should try to restructure their organizational functioning.
- PSBs should move from deposit orientation to profit orientation.

- In order to attract more and more customers, PSBs should become market savvy, but the cost of deposits and deployment plans should be kept in mind.
- In order to raise productivity and profitability PSBs should spell turnover strategies, income- oriented and cost-oriented strategies from time to time.
- PSBs should try to broad base the treasury functions to more centres in view of the growth of the financial sector.
- Now PSBs have started raising money from the capital market, so they should develop and integrate a formal shareholder value analysis in their planning process.
- Staffing and working patterns have to be reexamined from cost control point of view.
- Banks should develop the spirit of cost consciousness among its employees. It will also help in increasing the earnings.
- Better management information system, credit monitoring and cash management can result increase in productivity.
- In PSBs, low compensation is the biggest demotivator for the efficient employees. So it is suggested that the pay should be linked to individual performance, group performance and overall business result of the bank. Such a pay structure will motivate the employees.
- Committed staff especially in skill-oriented areas should be employed even by paying more, it will lead to higher productivity.
- Better coordination with the unions may give productivity, if the unions take a positive in matters relating to transfer, placement and technology upgradation.
- In Indian PSBs there is no clear cut placement and succession planning so in order to raise the productivity a well-defined succession plan will lead to smooth take over of important positions and it will result in a higher productivity.
- Banks should evolve strategies for handling the recovery of NPAs and they should also improve their asset quality. It is suggested that some major legal enactments should also be made in this regard.
- Banks should adopt scientific product pricing methods, effective asset liability management and risk management methods in order to raise their efficiency.

- PSBs should be given autonomy to manage their affairs. They should be free to recruit and promote staff and decide the type of personnel to choose for their needs even by paying more pay packages.
- PSBs should give comprehensive interpretation to innovative banking.
- PSBs should evolve effective cost standards. It will help them to reduce cost and, thus, raise earning.
- Timely SWOT analysis should be made. It will help the PSBs in improving their efficiency.
- In the PSBs decentralization of financial authority is needed. A change in the attitude of the bank babus should be affected to raise the productivity and profitability.

BRIEF OUTLINE OF THE RECOMMENDATIIONS OF THE COMMITTEE ON FINANCIAL SYSTEM (NARASIMHAM COMMITTEE - I - 1991)

- According to the committee the government intervention in Indian Banking Sector was in the form of high SLR. In this way, government promoted bank resources at below market rate. It benefited the government by reducing its cost of borrowings, thus reducing the profits of the banks. Therefore, the committee suggested that SLR should not be used for financing public sector. The committee recommended phased reduction in SLR from 38.5% in 1991 to 25% of the net demand, over the period of 5 years to leave more funds with the banks.

- Earlier CRR was used as a principle instrument of monitory and credit control. The committee recommended that RBI should relay on open market operations and should educe its dependence on CRR. According to the committee, the CRR should be reduced from the present high level

- be used regularly but in the extraordinary circumstances only. In order to support the weak sections of the society. The priority sector should be redefined to include marginal farmers, tiny, village, cottage industry, small business, transport operators, rural artisans and other weaker sections.

- The committee recommended that asset reconstruction fund should be set up to help the banks to take off bad and doubtful debt from their balance sheet and recycle the funds realized through this process into more productive uses.

- The committee recommended a board for financial supervision under the direct control of RBI should be setup.

- The committee recommended abolition of branch licensing. The committee suggested that the government should become more liberal with opening of branches of foreign banks in India. The government should not interfere in the internal organizations of the banks.

- The committee favoured less regulated system. It suggested more freedom should be given to banks to recruit officers.

- The committee recommended that duality of control over banks by RBI and banking division of the finance minister should be ended.

- The committee recommended for the adoption of uniform accounting practices mainly in regard to income recognition and provisioning against doubtful departments. The committee also recommended imparting for transparency of banks

- Balance Sheets. It suggested adoption of Ghosh committee guidelines for valuation of investments.

- The committee suggested reconstitution of banking system to have a few large banks, some national banks and local banks, by defining the jurisdiction of each and every bank.

- The committee suggested deregulation of interest rates. According to the committee, the interest rates should be market related. Banks should be free to offer varying rates of interest for different size of deposits.

- The committee suggested BIS norms in a phased manner particularly regarding CAR. The committee suggested that profitable banks should be allowed to raise funds from the capital market immediately.

- The committee suggested that DFIs should be granted operational flexibility and adequate internal autonomy. Cross equity holding amongst DSFIs should be done away with and various new guidelines relating to their working should be issued at the earliest.

Brief Outline of the Recommendations of the Committee on Banking Sector Reforms
(Narasimham Committee II - 1988)

- The committee recommended an increase in the minimum capital adequacy ratio to 9% by 2000 and further to 10% by 2002 by assigning 5% weightage for the government and other approved securities to hedge against market risk.

- The committee suggested that there should be a strong banking and financial system in order to have capital account convertibility.

- The committee recommended merger of strong banks with strong banks. It was against the merger of weak banks with strong banks. The committee suggested that weak banks should narrow down their operations to safer business.

- According to the committee the government was playing an excessive role in the functioning of the public sector banks. The committee suggested more autonomy and flexibility should be provided to these banks and government interference should be reduced.

- The committee suggested that lending operations of NBFCs should be integrated with the financial system. The NBFCs would get access to other forms of instruments in money market like treasury bills, bill discounting, commercial papers etc. It also suggested the opening of the treasury bill markets to foreign institutional investors

- The committee recommended a review and strengthening of the operations of the rural financial institutions in terms of appraisal, supervision and follow up, loan recovery and creating healthy relationships with the customers.

- The committee recommended that greater internal controls should be there as far as banking sector is concerned. The committee suggested that the regulatory and supervisory authorities should ensure transparency and creditability

- The committee recommended review of various Acts like RBI Act, SBI Act, Banker Book Evidence Act and Banking Companies Regulations Act.

- The committee suggested greater managerial autonomy to the public sector banks and reducing the government ownership in these banks. The committee suggested improvement in the recruitment practices of public sector banks. According to the committee the board of PSBs should be professionalized.

- The committee felt that there was an urgent need of utilizing information technology in the banking sector at the earliest.

- The committee suggested that effective system for asset liability management and risk management should be put in practice.

Brief Outline of the Recommendations of the Working Group for Harmonisation of the Operations of DFIs and Banks (Khan Committee - 1998)

- According to the committee, a super regulator should be there to coordinate the activities of other regulators.
- \
- The committee recommended redefining of the priority sector. It suggested change in the method of determining priority sector targets for financial institutions and banks. According to the committee infrastructure credit should be kept out of the net bank credit.

- The committee recommended that the time has come when the financial system of India should adopt universal banking.

- The committee favoured mergers between banks and banks, and banks and financial instituituions but it suggested that these mergers should be done in practical way and such reconstruction should be useful for the financial system as a whole.

- The company suggested that the various conditions on financial institutions regarding resource mobilization were against the interest of financial sector reforms and such a restrictions should be done away with.

- The committee suggested various changes in the state level financial institutions.

- The committee suggested the setting up of a coordination committee of banks and financial institutions to standardize the lending policies and quantity of credit.

- The committee recommended fast legal reforms in order to make quick recovery of loans.

- Another main recommendation of the committee was regarding reduction in CRR and elimination of SLR.

Brief Outline of the Recommendations Of the Working Group on Restructuring Weak Public Sector Banks

(Verma Committee - 1999)

The committee developed a four dimensional comprehensive programme for the restructuring of the weak public sector banks. The main areas were:

- Fist of all the committee emphasized on operational restructuring. The committee suggested that the banks should aim at increasing the income and by reducing their costs. The committee suggested that the banks should go into the lower and middle segment of the credit market. They should use ultra modern technology to compete with new private sector and foreign banks. The committee suggested that major problem of the public sector banks was mounting NPAs and it is

66

suggested a various ways to deal with this problem. The committee suggested that there is overstaffing in the public sector banks and it should be done away with at the earliest.

- As far as organizational restructuring is concerned, the committee suggested that unprofitable branches should be closed and there should be rationalization of the bank branches. The committee suggested that the CMD of a bank should be a capable person who can be appointed by giving more pay and perks. There should be two EDs to help the CMDs. The committee strongly recommended that proper training facilities should be provided to bank personnel and the government should not be provided to bank personnel and the government should not interfere in the working of these banks.

- The committee recommended that financial reconstruction is very much necessary the improvement in the functioning of the public sector banks. For this purpose, it suggested the establishment of Financial Restructuring Authority. The committee suggested that changes should be made in the working of debt recovery tribunals.

- The committee suggested systematic restructuring providing for legal changes and institutional building for aiding the entire restructuring process.

- In the Indian context, banking is really the proxy and indeed the corner stone of overall economic growth of the country. According to C.H. Bhabha, "Banking is the kingpin of the chariot of economic progress. As such its role in expanding economy of a country like India can neither be underestimated nor overlooked. The success of our plan is dependent among other things, on the smooth and satisfactory performance of the role by banking industry of our country." Banking is a service-oriented business requiring high levels of professional and personal skills and national boundaries are no longer relevant in mobilization and allocation of capital.

BIBLIOGRAPHY

- Jadhav, N. (1996), *Challenges to Indian Banking*, MacMillan India Ltd., Delhi Chapter – 32 p.279.
- Seethapathy, K and Bohini, K., "Indian Banking: Back to the future," *Analyst,* Feb.1999.
- Joshi, V.S. and Joshi V.V., *Managing Indian Banks: the Challenges Ahead,* 1998, Response Books, New Delhi.
- Selvaraj, V., "Challenges faced by Public Sector Banks," *Banking in the New Millennium,* Deep & Deep Publication, New Delhi.
- Jalan, Dr. Bimal, "Banking and Finance in the new Millinnium," *PNB Monthly Review,* Jan.2001.
- Kopleman, Richard E., *Managing Productivity Organizations.* McGraw Hill Book Company, New Delhi, 1986, p.3.
- Singh, Jagwant, "Productivity in the Indian Banking," A Thesis submitted to Panjab University, Chandigarh, Jan. 1990, p.54.
- Rao, C.B., "Productivity and competitiveness: A model for developing Economics," *ASCI Journal of Management,* Vol.23, No.2. March, 1994.
- Singh, Dr. Jagwant, "Productivity in Indian Banking", 1990. (A Thesis submitted to UBS Punjab University, Chandigarh).
- Desai, Vasant, *Principles of Bank Management,* (1991), Himalaya Publishing House.
- Godse, V.T., *Productivity in Banks – Concept and Measurements,* Papers presented at bank economists met. Madras, 1984, p.298.
- Dasgupta, Devajyoti, "Profitability of Indian Public Sector Banks in the light of liberalization of Indian Economy – An Overview," T*he Management Accountant,* Sept. 2001.
- Ramamoorthy, K.R., "Profitability and Productivity in Indian Banking," *Chartered Financial Analyst,* February 1998, p.53.
- Thomas, Z., "Performance Effectiveness of Nationalized Banks: A Case Study of Syndicate Bank," *Finance India,* Vol. XIV, No.1, March 2000, pp. 187-192.
- Khusro, A.M.,"Keynote Address *", BEM,* 1996, pp.1-19.
- Venkatratnam, M., *Social Objectives and Profitability of Commercial Banks,* Andhra Bank, Hyderabad, 1987.
- Bhubal, Subhash B., "Bank Profitability note worth the candle," *Indian Banking Today and Tomorrow,* Feb.1991.
- Krishna, Dr. R.R., "Profitability Analysis: an Overview," *Indian Banking Today and Tomorrow,* Sept. 1996.

www.ingramcontent.com/pod-product-compliance
Lightning Source LLC
Chambersburg PA
CBHW061839220326
41599CB00027B/5344